Advance praise for

Communities for Social Change

"Annette Coburn and Sinéad Gormally have produced a closely argued and well-illustrated text that shows a sound understanding of relevant theory and a sensitive appreciation of the situations of young people, communities and those who work with them. I recommend *Communities for Social Change* as a key text for policy makers, practitioners and those who research community and youth development."

—Ian Finlay, University of Oxford

"This book is very timely. It offers a critique of youth and community work informed by neo-liberal values and articulates an alternative vision based upon social justice. The contextual discussion relates mostly to the United Kingdom, but many ideas are transferable and hopefully this will prompt local adaptation in other contexts."

—Trudi Cooper, Edith Cowan University

"This is a timely and very useful book for anyone who is interested in young people's lives and issues of inequality and social justice. The book somewhat unusually blends theoretical insights with valuable discussion of innovative approaches to practice. It will be essential reading for anyone interested in challenging accepted ways of thinking about and working with young people."

—Tracy Shildrick, University of Leeds

Communities for Social Change

Studies in Criticality

Shirley R. Steinberg
General Editor

Vol. 483

The Counterpoints series is part of the Peter Lang Education list.
Every volume is peer reviewed and meets
the highest quality standards for content and production.

PETER LANG
New York • Bern • Frankfurt • Berlin
Brussels • Vienna • Oxford • Warsaw

Annette Coburn and Sinéad Gormally

Communities for Social Change

Practicing Equality and Social Justice in Youth and Community Work

PETER LANG
New York • Bern • Frankfurt • Berlin
Brussels • Vienna • Oxford • Warsaw

Library of Congress Cataloging-in-Publication Data

Names: Coburn, Annette, author. Gormally, Sinéad, author.
Title: Communities for social change: practicing equality and social justice
in youth and community work / Annette Coburn and Sinéad Gormally.
Description: New York, NY: Peter Lang, 2017.
Series: Counterpoints: studies in criticality; v. 483 | ISSN 1058-1634
Includes bibliographical references and index.
Identifiers: LCCN 2017015678 | ISBN 978-1-4331-2977-3 (hardcover: alk. paper)
ISBN 978-1-4331-2976-6 (paperback: alk. paper) | ISBN 978-1-4331-4440-0 (ebook pdf)
ISBN 978-1-4331-4441-7 (epub) | ISBN 978-1-4331-4442-4 (mobi)
Subjects: LCSH: Community education. | Community development.
Youth—Counseling of. | Social justice.
Classification: LCC LC1036 .C65 2017 | DDC 371.19—dc23
LC record available at https://lccn.loc.gov/2017015678
DOI 10.3726/b11265

Bibliographic information published by **Die Deutsche Nationalbibliothek**.
Die Deutsche Nationalbibliothek lists this publication in the "Deutsche
Nationalbibliografie"; detailed bibliographic data are available
on the Internet at http://dnb.d-nb.de/.

The paper in this book meets the guidelines for permanence and durability
of the Committee on Production Guidelines for Book Longevity
of the Council of Library Resources.

CONTENTS

ACKNOWLEDGMENTS

For Andy, David and Steven, and for Paddy and Ruairí – the people who give us reasons to smile every day and remind us why change is needed for the world to become a better place.

· 1 ·

INTRODUCTION

This chapter introduces the social structures, purpose and core ideas that underpin community work for equality and social justice. It considers core concepts and practices that inform why and how community and youth work (CYW) practitioners, and community members, are able to promote and develop social change. First, it contextualises our main concerns about working in a neo-liberal society that has shifted focus towards changing behaviours and the over-regulation of caring professions. In doing so, neoliberal ideology promotes compliance in taking forward punitive policies that stigmatize and individualise communities and young people (Giroux, 2009). This leads to discussion of the nature and purpose of CYW by offering a clear outline on what this means in the context of working with young people and communities. While drawing largely on research from the United Kingdom, the ideas and practice examples discussed will resonate with anyone involved in community and youth work as practitioner or participant, both inside and outside of the United Kingdom and Europe.

In critiquing routinised perspectives on resilience as an individual coping mechanism, we assert that community and youth workers should consider building and utilising community resilience that, as a more collective and social endeavour, can be used to resist and to challenge dominant discourses and positively impact on the lived experiences of people who experience inequality and injustice. The chapter also outlines a distinctive and clear epistemological stance that relates to CYW practices. The possibility for readers to utilise their own experiences and research insights, in addition to those presented here, can help to facilitate praxis among a wider international Community of Practice (Lave and Wenger, 1991; Wenger, 1998; Wenger and Traynor, 2015). This seeks to increase capacity for achieving a good life (Sen, 1985) by strengthening a critical and higher purpose of emancipatory practice that is constructed around CYW practices, and strives for social justice and equality.

Neo-liberal Impacts on Young People and Community Work

Historically, the Chicago School of Sociology was prominent in researching the development of subcultures where, 'material deprivation, physical decay and the tough cultural environment of the inner city influenced children in such areas towards delinquency' (O'Donnell, 1997, p. 350). Yet, while raising concerns about poverty, this also constructed a pathologising and generalising discourse of young people as delinquent and of communities in need of reform, something we need to be aware of and critique.

The pervasiveness of age as a regulating factor, particularly in young people's lives, is a recurring theme in sustaining this pathology. While our analysis in this chapter draws largely on examples from literature in youth work or youth studies, we believe that similar concerns can also be identified in the experiences of older people and children, or indeed any other age category. As a social construct, the idea of age, as a means of determining status, developing services, or in defining identity, is something of a conundrum – having some utility as a way of organising society but it is not always relevant in a community context or in real-life settings where people's experiences of discrimination and injustice are based on entirely different constructs, such as ability, gender, race or religion. So, in considering discourse on youth and young people we are clear that the following critique may also be applied to conditions and discourses that are experienced across an extended age range and in different social groups.

Mizen (2004) has shown that the political restructuring of the state, since the late 1970s has, in the United Kingdom, compounded the problem of exclusion. Using age as a means of social division is integral to the neo-liberal market-driven economies that have replaced the UK's Keynesian welfare state. In this way, young people's aspirations have become limited through a policy environment where 'age provides the means through which traditional sources of inequality between the young can be reproduced' (Mizen, 2004, p. 22). This is especially cogent in the United Kingdom, and elsewhere in the Western world, where a persistent policy discourse takes a negative and pathologising view of young people and where, 'the trickle of stories about youth work is in inverse proportion to the flood of stories about youth' (Batsleer, 2010, p. 154). This discourse is further exemplified in research and literature about gangs, which is critiqued as gang-talk (Hallsworth and Young, 2008), a discourse which perpetuates a range of myths about gangs and maintains a pathologising view of young people who choose to hang around the streets but are not 'in-gangs' (see Gormally and Deuchar, 2012; Gormally, 2015).

In the United States and further afield, Giroux (2005; 2009) argues that the conditions in which young people live are often masked by influences, such as the media and patriarchal or colonial inheritances, that impact on families, young people and the arrangements for education. Argued as evident in the, 'widespread adoption of … values, policies and symbolic practices that legitimate forms of organised violence … [as a] … culture of cruelty' (Giroux, 2012, p. 14), this creates and sustains policies that, 'humiliate and punish … [and] … deal with problems that would be better addressed through social reforms rather than punishment' (p. 15). Giroux further asserts neoliberal culture as one where it is easy for people to:

> … turn away from the misfortunes of others and respond with indifference to the policies and practices of truly corrupt individuals and institutions of power that produce huge profits at the cost of massive suffering and social hardship.
>
> Giroux (2012, p. 16)

One example of this kind of culture of cruelty has evolved in Britain through the ways in which the poorest communities, across all ages, have been negatively impacted by changes in social welfare (Beatty and Fothergill, 2013). Placing 'conditionality and responsibility at the heart of welfare policy' (Beatty et al, 2015, p. IV), and at the heart of reform, the main focus was to increase the severity and length of sanctions in order to change behaviour, and where, according to Beatty and Fothergill (2013), the poorest areas in Britain were hit the hardest. Beatty et al (2015) linked the impact of benefit sanctions to food poverty, survival crime, family/relationship tensions, mental and physical health problems, fuel poverty, debt and disengagement from the welfare system. They also found that in adding to the problems homeless people face, benefit sanctions may actually increase the risk of homelessness, while Griggs and Evans (2010) also reported for the Joseph Rowntree Foundation a link between higher sanction rates and 'personal barriers'.

In reviewing the Welfare Reform Act (2010), Oakley (2014) identified, 'that only 23% of claimants who said their benefit had been stopped or reduced said they had been told about hardship payments' (p. 9). Although finding that the system was not 'broken', as had often been claimed in political rhetoric (Blair, 1995; Cameron, 2005 as cited in Thorp and Kennedy, 2010), the Oakley review identified room for improvement as many claimants did not fully understand the requirements put upon them and the details of the sanctioning process:

> ... claimants can be unaware of where sanctions referrals originated from and who to speak to about them. This can result in claimant concerns and queries being passed "from pillar to post" with little hope of resolution.
>
> Oakley (2014, p. 10)

Another example of how a culture of cruelty persists among adults is exemplified in research about the 'narrative journey of discovery and recovery from a fat, middle-aged, and single woman' (Beierling, 2014, p. 256). This narrative explores the persistence of negative and oppressive experiences among women whose experiences of popular culture meant that their physical size, in comparison with thin women, brought 'ridicule, scorn, and disgust ... [where rude comments] ... were hurtful, and each built upon the other, casting my own self-worth deeper into the shadows' (p. 261). Beierling concluded that 'weight prejudice really does exist' (p. 261). This prejudice is driven by dominant discourses, often grounded in profit-seeking powerful cultural industries, that create normalised images of what a woman should look like in order to 'fit in' and which silence the voices of those who do not conform to the dominant social conditions that are apparent in popular culture.

These examples reveal powerful negative discourses in policy reform and popular culture. Yet, while such discourses persist, alternative positions can be taken, and the need for dissent (Martin, 2001) is revealed as an important means of challenging the status quo, in order for new discourses, and ways of being, to emerge. Making experiences of popular culture visible (both positive and negative aspects) and encouraging the articulation of positive experiences and silenced voices, creates possibilities for problem posing education.

Problem posing is crucial to the creation of powerful learning environments (De Corte et al., 2003; Konings et al., 2005) by involving learners in grappling with real problems that are challenging and complex and in the process of creating new knowledge and unforeseen ideas. Offering spaces for people to learn with and from each other through informal social educational environments is important in community development.

Taking popular culture and lived experience as the starting point for conversation and dialogue, creates possibilities for powerful learning about difference and power relations in ways that are authentic, challenging and complex, and where opportunities to refine or shift discourse become, not only possible, but also probable. Such environments offer and create alternative discourses that are affirming and positive, rather than being primarily negative and oppressive. They are a catalyst for liberating and hopeful pedagogy that is concerned with critical conversation and powerful engagement.

According to Steinberg and others (Darder, Baltodano and Torres, 2009; Giroux, 2009; Kincheloe, 2008) an analysis of the pedagogical power of popular culture, requires a rethinking of education both inside and outside of schooling, and across cultures and communities. For example, Steinberg (2011) has examined developments in popular culture and the corporate construction of childhood to suggest that these have combined with technological advances to open up young people's access to the adult world, whereby:

> technology ... does not determine everyday life ... it interacts with a variety of social and cultural contexts and drives individual agents to produce interactive social process ... [that] ... has produced profound—but not uniform—social changes.
>
> Steinberg (2011, p. 37)

This suggests a paradox in the utility of technology as both friend and foe of the rich and poor, oppressor and oppressed. Thus, without careful rethinking, of what this on-line interactive social process means for education, and what kind of professional educator is now required, the influence of global corporations in schooling and in popular culture could serve as a hegemonic foundation that shores up materialism and sustains the neoliberal project. Rather, it is vital to promote and create spaces that can support the generation of alternative ways of thinking and being, in developing a new world view on equality and social justice. In this regard, Aronowitz (2009) has suggested that 'schools should cut their ties to corporate interests and reconstruct the curriculum along the lines of intellectual endeavour' (p. 120). The need for alternative thinking was also evident in practices where corporate sponsorship underpinned the build-up to the 2012 Olympic Games and the 2014 Commonwealth Games. Both the UK and Scottish Governments promoted a particularly 'hands-on' approach to involving business partners in schools as part of a wider drive to promote enterprise and entrepreneurship among students. This suggested that:

> … business involvement in schools reflects a series of priorities in respect of the economic climate of the 21st Century and its dominant ideological proclivities.
> Coburn and McCafferty (2016, p. 27)

In this way corporate sponsorship of major sporting events serves to maintain the neoliberal condition and allows multinational corporations to develop their cultural and economic reputations, even in settings (such as schools) where product placement is routinely banned. In 2012, Coca-Cola's connection with the Olympics included sponsorship of the Olympic Torch relay, which involved high profile media coverage over 70 days in the build-up to the Games, and also the 'Real Business Challenge' involving schools across the country, for two years prior to the event, in designing an education centre as part of the Games' legacy.

While this access to young people's minds may be worrying, the problem of corporate involvement in education goes much deeper than simple sponsorship or working in schools to collaborate on development of business and enterprise skills, in order to secure future employment. The problem of corporate involvement lies in the pervasive extent to which education itself has become a marketable commodity where:

> … students are being subjected to a stripped-down notion of schooling … Shaped by a pedagogy of containment, security and conformity that undermines critical thought, teaching and dialogue … [and] … emphasises market values.
> Giroux (2012, p. 51)

This is not confined solely to school students, as the problem of corporate involvement is part of an on-going issue for education within capitalist society, whereby:

> … young people, especially those from the most disadvantaged contexts, are being 'consumed' by capitalism … [in schools that] … are being swept into the neoliberal

project of constructing themselves as unmitigated zones of marketization (mostly of themselves against other schools) in order to secure the market share'.

Smyth (2014, p. 69)

Neo-liberal drivers in public policy and management of services have also regulated educational youth work practice, for example, through the introduction of market driven, business practices and a focus on accreditation of individual performance. This is evidenced in a function-by-function set of competences and the creation of occupational standards for youth work (LLUK, 2008). The LLUK standards document includes 200 pages that offer an extensive list of basic standards and competencies such as, being able to 'communicate effectively and develop rapport with young people' or to 'identify and secure resources for youth work.' Yet, they also include some more complex elements, such as 'lead change' or 'support young people in taking action and tackling problems'.

While not in themselves problematic, there is little to be gained in using statistical or business methods to measure such complex areas. The reduction of people as learners to measurable outputs is a fallacy—learners of all ages, do not arrive in educational settings as empty vessels, ready to be filled with knowledge and to develop new skills or understanding (Freire, 1996). Thus, when examining the state of CYW in contemporary policy environments, the introduction of outcome-focussed policies could be seen in a positive light, providing direction and demonstrating value for money, or in negative light, could be seen as constraining practice to a limiting set of competences, or in leading to the creation of competences that are so wide-ranging they become meaningless. Development of such policies also reduces flexibility in reshaping relationships between youth workers and young people (Davies and Merton, 2009).

Davies and Merton (2009) argued that a shift from non-accredited informal learning toward accredited qualifications could also be regarded as a positive move in helping young people to find work. However, they temper this counter argument by highlighting that this shift is most productive when it flows organically, from the youth work process, rather than being introduced as a specific purpose of the programme (Davies and Merton, 2009). This emphasises the voluntary or negotiated nature of engagement in youth work, as distinct from engagement that is tied to, for example, payment or receipt of benefits. Yet, increasingly the routine practice of surveillance inside youth work (Coburn, 2011) is problematic in positioning adults as being in authority over young people and as such, potentially stifles possibilities for creativity, freedom and for participants and practitioners to take responsibility for development of the youth work setting.

All of this suggests that, as state intervention in the lives of young people has increased (Mizen, 2004), youth work has become 'increasingly prescriptive, intrusive and insistent' (Davies and Merton, 2009, p. 46). This raises questions about the future development and funding of youth work, and whether the kind of youth work that puts the young person at the centre of a social and democratic process will remain. A targeting of outcomes and outputs related to behaviour change, to preparation for work or diversion from prosecution, suggests a purpose for youth work that may constrain its emancipatory purpose for social change. This kind of interventionist approach to behaviour change seems to be a step too far in fostering compliance with, and acceptance of, existing orthodoxies, rather than developing a process through which the circumstances that have prompted such behaviour or created those orthodoxies can be challenged and changed.

Considering the extent to which young people have become consumed by capitalism brings important aspects of self-esteem and self-worth to the forefront of thinking about young people's lived experience. If such attributes are tied to a materialist view, young people who experience poverty and inequality may resort to behaviours that are not acceptable or desirable in a fair and democratic society. Yet, such behaviour is often influenced by unfair and undemocratic processes that operate within contemporary society in order to maintain the status quo and sustain inequality and injustice. Thus, rather than needing to 'change behaviour' if we are serious about equality and social justice we need to change the world and to challenge the structural and hegemonic processes that silence or ignore the poorest and most excluded communities.

We believe that CYW can contribute to the change process. Yet, Jeffs and Banks (2010) suggest that an agenda of social control has become more explicit and dominant and this affects the methods used to engage with young people, while also creating an increasingly controlling purpose for youth work. Similarly, Fyffe (2010) warns against tokenistic forms of participation that could serve to exclude rather than engage young people in citizenship activity or in critical, problem posing activity, which is vital in addressing aspects of equality and social justice (Coburn and Gormally, 2015).

We are concerned that in seeking to prescribe or predict outcomes, a singular focus for youth work is created in regard to the content of the programme delivered (What youth work does?), and in its informal approach or methodology (How youth work is developed?). This shifts focus away from the important question of its underpinning values and purpose (Why youth work is?) This shifting focus means that the values and purposes of youth work as emancipatory or democratic may be assumed as part of its 'informal process' that is overtly interested in questions of what and how, without seriously interrogating or asserting those aspects of practice, 'as a process' for social change, that is overtly interested in driving social change.

Of course, what we do and how we do it are important in the development of practice and in scoping professional or practice boundaries. However, without its distinctive value-base in emancipatory and democratic purpose, educational youth work may be reduced to the kind of leisure time pursuit that Banks (2010) has alerted us to, or to the role of short-term fixer of deficiencies in employability, parenting or suchlike. This kind of practice delivers youth work as a product to consumers, rather than developing youth work as an educational process that is achieved through dialogue and in association with young people. The questions raised here make it important to consider what we actually mean when we talk about community and youth work.

The Nature and Purpose of Community and Youth Work (CYW)

The position taken by Sercombe (2010) defines youth work by its focus on the young person, as the primary client in their social contexts. When the young person is the primary concern of practice, 'this places youth work in radical distinction to most other forms of engagement with young people … [where the role] … is to balance the various interests of different stakeholders' (Sercombe, 2010, p. 26). This seems to offer a reasonable way of distinguishing youth work from other professions but the idea of primary client is contested in its use of 'client' to describe the relationship between youth worker and young person. This lack of consensus is indicative of an emerging or maturing youth work profession, exemplified in the introduction of specialised training as recently as the 1960s. We have argued that youth work is now in a liminal state internationally (Coburn and Gormally, 2015a), defined as:

> A time when the old configurations of social reality are increasingly seen to be in jeopardy, but new alternatives are not yet in hand … liminality is a safe place in

which to host such ambiguity, to notice the tension and unresolved without pressure, but with freedom to see and test alternative textings of reality.

Brueggemaan (1995, pp. 319–20)

In light of this liminality, we recognise a shift in social realities for youth work and youth workers where contemporary conversations are testing alternative ideas on the nature and purpose of practice. For example, proposing youth work as education, Harland and McCready (2012) assert the need for professional equity across educational methodologies (inside and outside of schools). Although the work of Sercombe (2010) and Harland and McCready (2012) is contextualised in youth work, we believe that the kind of educational methodology, in which participant situations or interests are the primary focus of the learning relationship, can also be applied to adult education and community development contexts.

For example, in contemporary research and literature, the creation of supportive relationships among workers and participants in community based adult learning (CBAL) was found to be important in creating social capital and enhanced feelings of well-being (McIntyre, 2014). Similarly, in a community development context Shaw (2008) highlights inherent tensions that exist, when working with communities amidst increasing expectations that practitioners will 'deliver' policy and measure outputs that have become more important than social and democratic purpose. Proposing a 'non-negotiable' social and moral focus, Shaw asserts a purpose for community development practice 'to work alongside people in communities to assist them in thinking about and articulating their own, often contradictory, experience of policy, and in taking action around their collective interest and concerns' (p. 16).

This demonstrates a value-laden and purposeful educational relationship that underpins CYW practice, whereby workers are committed to engaging with people in communities, on their own terms, across a variety of contexts. CYW is thus, not limited by socially constructed age distinctions, nor by the constraints of ever-changing policy directives—although it may be loosely organised around such distinctions, these are not essential elements of the work. Instead, as we assert throughout this book, the purpose of CYW as a social and moral endeavour, that explores how we can work with communities in order to facilitate development of a fairer, more equal and socially just, society. Putting people and communities first, means that community and youth workers always see the primary focus of practice as, 'an ethical commitment to serve' (Sercombe, 2010, p. 10) and where grassroots practice, 'should involve collective educational practice derived from the social reality of people in communities' (Shaw, 2008, p. 16).

To facilitate discussion on the methodologies of practice, while also retaining important aspects of earlier developmental experiences, we have already proposed border pedagogy as a threshold concept for realising new configurations of methodological praxis across a range of professional contexts (Coburn and Gormally, 2015). We return to this proposal in Chapter 9, but for now, it is useful to introduce the idea of focussing practice in and across professional borderlands. This is important in working with communities and people who experience parallel or shifting contexts because crossing borders can help to create new possibilities for CYW.

Throughout this book, we argue for retention of distinct practices but we also draw on research findings and practice experiences that might help to reshape and reconfigure practice that fits well within a range of contemporary contexts. This does not mean that we are advocating compliance with neo-liberal drivers that have reduced education to a functional commodity. It simply means that we recognise the complexities of practice within shifting environments and, as an emancipatory practice seeking to respond to the current onslaught of neoliberalism, we identify a need to revisit aspects of practice that were previously firmly fixed, such as the voluntary principle in youth work, in order to reimagine possibilities for future development. Again, while much of our argument here relates directly to youth work, we see relevance to all CYW practices.

Youth work has evolved over the last 150 years to meet various educational, social, cultural and political needs (Jeffs and Smith, 2010). In the United Kingdom, youth workers are presently employed in areas such as education, health, employment, community safety and in participation, and citizenship activity. Yet, in particular, their capacity to adapt in order to meet current demands for services that prioritise safety and economic wealth has, according to Davies (2005; 2012) left some forms of youth work vulnerable to misinterpretation.

There is vigorous debate about the nature and purpose of youth work, which has increasingly been described as under-threat (de St Croix, 2010; Taylor, 2008; Young, 2006). Despite a reduction in the volume of open and accessible youth clubs across the United Kingdom, Robertson (2005) makes a convincing argument for youth club work. Arguing that youth clubs should be developed in tandem with other community provision, as free-standing facilities or as a part of the local community based provision for adults, families and children, Robertson (2005) offers enhanced value for youth club work as part of wider community provision. This coheres with the Scottish context for youth work, which is situated within a Community Education tradition and where the emergence of a Curriculum for Excellence has underpinned the evolution of a national agency for youth work, called YouthLink Scotland. This advocates and promotes a single youth work sector, incorporating community, public and voluntary sectors working collaboratively for the good of all young people. This is not always the case across the United Kingdom— where sectors are discrete and often set in competition to each other.

Community Education was established in Scotland, in response to the Alexander Report (SED, 1975) which proposed a combined adult education and youth work service to create locally driven adult education, community development and youth work, supported by interagency collaboration. The explicit aim of Alexander was to:

> ... create a more relevant curriculum within communities ... that would stimulate participation in education ... [with] ... an important part to play in nurturing a pluralist democracy by helping to manage the tension between the policies of the state and the politics of communities.
>
> Tett (2010, p. 18)

This ethos remains as a driver of practice in the Community Learning and Development (CLD) sector (Tett, 2010) where practices in adult education, community development and youth work are aligned as domains of community education practice. Taken in the broadest sense, this sector embraces voluntary and statutory agencies, organisations and national policies and in doing so, cuts across all age groupings.

Literature shows that adult education and youth work are less structured and more informal than, for example, schooling or traditional evening classes, and are often developed as 'social purpose education' (Martin, 2007, p. 10), underpinned by community development principles within the wider community education frame. This sees participants as social actors engaged in dialogue to promote social change. Yet, in each of the four UK nations, these three domains have developed quite different strategic visions for future practice and social policy, where there has been progress in rearticulating a social and democratic purpose for youth work (Coburn and Wallace, 2011; Jeffs and Smith, 2005; Tett, 2010) and in defending youth work in response to the challenges of global recession and austerity (Davies, 2011; Taylor, 2008; 2010).

Community development is routinely aligned with youth work in the teaching of professionally validated programmes. Recently the University of Hull was the first undergraduate degree in England to seek professional endorsement from both the National Youth Agency and The *Endorsement and Quality Standards Board* for *Community Development* Learning (ESB). The demand from practitioners and recognition from academics that the landscape for youth work is changing has meant that practice is varied and not often conducted in open access, specifically designed, youth work centres. Rather practice can take place in a variety of settings and under numerous guises. Our assertion would be that good community development practice should include young people and good youth work practice should recognise that young people come from families and communities that need to be worked alongside in striving for social change. This shift in practice can lead to debates about what is, and is not, youth work or community development practice.

For example, in an exploratory study of youth workers' perceptions and experiences of youth work in Northern Ireland (Harland and Morgan, 2006) suggested that, 'there seemed to be more consensus ... [about] ... what youth work was *not*' (p. 8). In Northern Ireland and Scotland, we find, as practitioners and in our research, that youth work is aligned to and underpinned by wider community development principles but we are aware that this is not always the case. Historically, practice has tended to be configured more discretely as either youth work or community development and also, as either statutory or voluntary sector provision. Thus, the nature and purpose of youth work remains complex and contested. This lack of consensus, is also demonstrated in the almost universal acceptance, across the United Kingdom, of the voluntary principle as a defining feature of youth work where voluntary participation, as distinct from being required or referred to attend, has been used to distinguish educational youth work from practices that take place in schools, prisons, or other settings (Davies, 2005, 2015; Jeffs and Smith, 2010; Young, 2006).

Yet, this principle may be compromised when young people attend because they are required in law, as in school-based practice. It may also be compromised if young people participate only because their friends do, or because it is affordable, or if there are no local alternatives. In a study of how young people learned about equality in youth work, Coburn (2012) found that, while the voluntary principle was important, participation was also mediated by a range of factors outwith the youth work setting, such as peer groups, family relationships or availability in terms of access, location and costs. It is therefore important at the outset to establish whether decisions to participate are ever based on a fair and free choice and to question whether there are circumstances in which it is possible that the voluntary principle might be compromised, yet the encounter could still be called youth work. For example, if the negotiated aspects of relationship building in youth work are brought to the fore, the voluntary principle need not be a 'deal-breaker' (Coburn and Gormally, 2015) in whether something is defined as youth work or not.

Further, it has also been argued that generic activity, as distinct from targeted intervention, might be discounted as youth work altogether, to avoid confusing a broad range of leisure time pursuits with youth work as a distinct disciplinary area or specialist occupation (Banks, 2010). Yet, Banks goes on to suggest that youth work can be regarded as a specialist occupation which involves, 'work with young people with an informal and/or developmental approach and purpose ... by people who are qualified as youth workers or who consciously adopt the identity of youth worker' (Banks, 2010, p. 5). This developmental purpose is foundational to our synthesis of community and youth work and is dependent on what Harland and Morgan (2006) have asserted as a 'process of youth work ... [this is] ... contingent on the quality of relationship between a young person and a youth worker' (Harland and Morgan, 2006, p. 10).

In this way, youth work is understood as being different from generic leisure time activity. It is set within the context of informal education and where young people engage with someone who is conscious to their identity as youth worker. This is often set within bespoke youth work settings and in the context of young people's leisure time but may also be developed in wider community contexts where the negotiated nature of relationships is clearly understood and visible (Coburn and Gormally, 2015). Regardless of setting, youth work needs to be attractive enough to sustain young people's choice to participate and thus, is different from other practices that take an informal approach to working with people of a particular age, or identified as 'youth'. Not all work with young people should be described as youth work simply because of the age of the people involved.

We define this kind of work in the following statement: *Youth work is practiced in settings where leisure time space and activity are often, yet not exclusively, the social context in which qualified and critically conscious youth workers engage with young people in order to develop a professional relationship that is grounded in a social and democratic educational purpose of change and transformation.*

Youth work can be developed in an informal social context, where there is a mix of open access activity that can be a catalyst for the development of more specialist or project-based work. Youth work can also include a range of projects and programmes in contexts where relationships are negotiated with and by young people in order to create a dynamic, flexible and informal, learning environment. Youth work is therefore simultaneously cultural, educational, social and political, and the young person is always the primary client.

This argument holds good in relation to the term community and youth work (CYW) as it encompasses practices that may include formal and informal contexts such as those that are in keeping with community education or community development principles, and where the focus of the work is always a value laden, social and moral activity. It involves working with people on their own terms and in their current social contexts. We use CYW to denote work across three core domains of practice, where community development values underpin educational practices in youth work and adult education that may incorporate programmed, or prescribed activity but is always open to renegotiation and reshaping by participants, in order to bring about social transformation. While recognising these three core domains of adult education, community development and youth work, our inclination is to widen the scope of practices to embrace contemporary and increasingly targeted CYW such as, family learning, literacies work, work with older people, health improvement or digital inclusion and well-being. Having examined perspectives on CYW, we now turn to the contextualisation of practice in which equality and social justice are a main driver.

The Context for Equality Work

The word equality has different meanings for different people. Equality has been identified as concerned with equipping people to have the capacity to deal with their own situations and to make decisions that enable them to take forward their own aims and actions (Baker et al., 2004; 2009). When people are connected by a shared or common identity, or when they interact with each other in a particular or systematic way, they are often identified as a social group. Members of a social group share the privilege or disadvantage that comes with belonging to the group, and in life, people often belong to a number of social groups on the basis, for example, of gender, class or race (Giddens, 2003).

The study of social groups and their experiences of inequality can be described as equality studies. Baker et al. (2004) have also argued equality studies as interdisciplinary and transformative, in the same way that women's studies and disability studies work across disciplinary boundaries to transform how the world is understood in order to promote equality. Baker et al. (2004, p. 42) have suggested that in studying equality, 'it is often useful to focus on particular ... social groups because individuals usually experience inequality as a consequence of their membership of these groups'. Equality is also understood as a relational concept applied to both individuals and to groups (Wyn and Whyte, 1997). However, the level and purpose of those relationships are complex and difficult to define. For example, everyone having their basic needs met does not mean meeting these needs equally for each person.

Thus, young people's capacity to deal with their own situations is influenced by how they are positioned in relationship to the rest of society and to each other. In the United Kingdom, the balance of power is routinely held by controlling adults who see young people as 'a threat to the social fabric of this country' (Barber, 2007, p. 79). In this way, adult control over young people is assumed and has led to their exclusion from political and social processes that sometimes make it difficult for them to assert their rights as citizens (Bessant, 2007; de St. Croix, 2010; Taylor, 2010). This makes it difficult for young people to take forward their own aims and actions. In effect, young people may be regarded as a social group that experiences inequality because of the pervasiveness of age as a means of organising and achieving status in contemporary society. Of course as they grow older their experiences of age-based discrimination subsides. However, by then it may be too late to overcome their experiences or feelings of powerlessness or lack of autonomy in life choice.

This differentiation of people by age is a relatively new phenomenon. According to Smith (1988) such differentiation was developed in some industrial societies to categorise people for institutional and policy purposes. Mizen (2004) cites Parsons (1942) and Eisenstadt (1956) to suggest that since the middle of the twentieth century age categorisations have been used increasingly to determine entitlements to education or welfare benefits. Mizen (2004) proposes that using age as a means of organising society is not in itself problematic but suggests that the assumption of adult power over children and young people is concerning. To understand this concern, we needed to examine more closely how this assumption has prevailed.

In Western societies, the concept of adolescence was constructed in the early 1900s by G. Stanley Hall and became synonymous with thinking about a period of growth from childhood to adulthood, often viewed as troublesome (Jeffs and Smith, 2005; 2010). This thinking informed early youth work development by responding to young people's apparent need to negotiate a difficult period in their lives. This assumes that young people need to engage in a series of personal and staged challenges, in the shift from childhood to adulthood. These challenges are suggested as a developmental process that young people go through to achieve physical and physiological changes in, for example, puberty, becoming independent from parents/carers and developing their own set of values and beliefs (Green, 2010).

While Young (2006) suggests that focussing on a specific age range and the concept of adolescence are important in youth work, adolescence is not a universal phenomenon and young people's experiences vary between generations (Green, 2010). The concept is therefore fragile and disputed. Epstein (2007) suggests that many of the problems young people face are a result of the adolescent construct, rather than a phenomenon that is explained by a theory of adolescence. So, despite its dominance in literature for over 100 years, the place of adolescence in informing the nature and purpose of youth work may be questioned in some fields or within particular discourses.

This appears to be the case in youth work discourse where it is suggested that those who are seriously interested in young people do not use the term adolescence because it is taken as 'a signal that the young people being referred to are … objectified, categorised and judged' (Wyn and White, 1997, p. 56). The concept has created an overemphasis on biological development as underpinning the process of 'growing up'. The term adolescence has been suggested as 'a period of physical, sexual and emotional development occurring between the ages of about 12 and 18' (Furlong and Cartmel, 2007, p. 55) and as such, also covers a limited time span.

Persistent use of the term adolescence as an important stage in young people's development, has also been described as 'worse than useless, designed … to detect normality and deviance, health and illness' when suggested as a fixed and homogeneous process (Batsleer, 2008, p. 51). Yet, the prevalence of this concept contributes to constructions of young people as deficient, not-quite-whole beings. This view is exemplified in persistent differences in how young people are treated, compared to adults.

Jeffs and Smith (1999) provide an interesting example that illustrates how age-specific language differentiates people and expresses the power of adults over young people. They used the example of truancy (unauthorised absence from school) to illustrate this differential. Truancy is routinely regarded as a serious problem among young people, often leading to formal sanction or punishment in school or local authority contexts. Yet, they highlight that truancy is not confined to young people. For example, by using the language of absenteeism (unauthorised absence from work) this could be regarded as an adult problem too. They suggest that absenteeism is not regarded, or responded to, in the same way as truancy. They propose that using different language to describe absence such as truancy or absenteeism is indicative of a negative discourse that defines young people as a social problem that is not consistently applied to the adult population (Jeffs and Smith, 1999).

Theorising of youth as a period of transition (Cohen, 1997) is less reliant than adolescence on the use of age as a signifier of staged development. Transitions theory suggests that young people become adult through their engagements with institutional structures (Furlong and Cartmel, 2007). For example, in the transition from school to work or from family to independent life, gender or class, are more influential than age (MacDonald and Marsh, 2005).

Transition is discussed in terms of life trajectories that suggest young people's choices about what happens to them are limited. However, it has been argued that some transitions may be more difficult than others, depending on individual or economic circumstances (Furlong and Cartmel, 2007). This has led to increased involvement by youth workers in, for example, jobs access or parenting work, in order to help young people successfully navigate their transitions (MacDonald and Marsh, 2005; Roberts, 2011). This kind of youth work may be helpful in mitigating structural influences and the concept of a fixed trajectory. However, the idea of youth transitions can also bring confusion.

For example, while the categorisation of young people as being 'in transition' offers a fluid view of the period between childhood and adulthood, seeing young people as both dependent children and independent adults, has also led to confusion. It is suggested that, 'different government departments construct youth in different ways, ... [and so] ... some policy messages are therefore contradictory' (Jones and Bell, 2000, p. 1). If there is inconsistency in how young people are regarded in policy, this affects how practices are developed. Added to this, the introduction of new public management methods has fostered compliance in meeting targets related to the number of young people who achieve outputs in predetermined outcomes (Davies and Merton, 2009; Harland and Morgan, 2006). Thus, while the concept of transition is useful it is also complex.

The UN Convention (United Nations, 1989) that asserts the rights of children and young people to be included in decision making about matters that affect them has led to the inclusion of young people in development of local and national strategic policies on youth and youth work by seeking to empower young people through involving them in decision making. In Scotland, the Youth Enquiry Service established in the 1980's (Strathclyde Regional Council, 1984), laid the foundations for more recent developments such as Young Scot and the first sitting of the Scottish Youth Parliament in 1999 (Scottish Youth Parliament, 2008), with a UK Youth Parliament following in 2001.

Although the involvement of young people in participation networks may be individually beneficial, McCulloch (2007) has argued that their participation does not appear to facilitate significant change in how they are viewed by society or in how they are involved in democratic processes. Further, Harland, Harvey, Morgan and McCready (2005) confirm that policy developments have created an 'ideological shift' (p. 58) that has fragmented the sector, as youth work became aligned with a deficit view of young people (Barber, 2007; Morgan and O'Hare, 2001; Waiton, 2001) with, according to Tett (2006), a focus on 'deficiencies and lack of responsibility rather than their marginality or the impact of structural inequalities on their lives' (p. 49).

Yet, there is nothing new in the drive toward age-dependent fixes, for example, in critiquing short-term programmes to resolve problems associated with economic and individual exclusion, Milburn et al. (1995) suggested that the breadth of the youth work curriculum was constrained by a focus on delivery of products, rather than development of processes. Yet, one of its earliest and most ardent supporters described the youth club as:

> ... a society of personalities with a community sense, which is the essence of good citizenship .... We are not concerned with the making of 'good club members' or 'well-organized youth groups', but with a much wider issue, the making of good citizens. This can only be done in a society where each member is important, where each one is given a chance to contribute something to the life of the group - the leader no more and no less than the member. It is for this reason that self-government is so important in club work.
>
> McAlister-Brew (1943, p. 12)

Despite being written in the 1940s, this serves as an important reminder about the emancipatory purpose of youth work. More recently, and at European level, a White Paper entitled A New Impetus for Youth (European Commission, 2001) gathered data from all member states to suggest a positive construction of young people:

The strongest message given by young people is their will to play an active part in the society in which they live. If they are excluded, democracy is not being allowed to function properly. They regard the view that they are disinterested or uncommitted as groundless and unjust. They feel that they are given neither the resources nor the information and training that would enable them to play a more active role.

European Commission (2001, p. 24)

This evidence suggested that young people wanted to be actively involved in society, but felt more could be done to help them become involved. The White Paper argued for a range of formal and informal methods to be developed to encourage participation and to create opportunities for young people to learn skills for effective participation.

Five years later, the European Youth Forum argued that the creation of a 'culture of participation' was a missing link in achieving a more socially just Europe (European Union, 2006). Thus, while youth participation appears to have permeated youth policy development across member states in the European Union, in the United Kingdom a deficit model of young people has been argued as persistent in the development of youth policy and youth work policy (Davies and Merton, 2009; Shaw and McCulloch, 2009). This remains particularly problematic in a post-Brexit UK and anywhere that such narratives persist in regard to young people and communities or social groups that are perceived as different.

At present, a range of policies have sought to address young people's deficiencies as the starting point for development of services. For example, the reports entitled Promoting Positive Outcomes: Working Together to Prevent Antisocial Behaviour in Scotland (Scottish Government, 2011a; 2009) were critical of earlier assumptions that enforcement should be the main thrust of policy intervention on Anti-Social Behaviour (ASB). This introduced a policy that sought a 'shared vision for how anti-social behaviour should be tackled' (2009, p. 7). On one hand this assumes that certain behaviour that young people engage in is antisocial and needs a strategic response but on the other hand, policy has also shifted towards the creation of opportunities that 'encourage more balanced and evidence-based reporting and counter negative stereotypes and the demonization of young people in the media' (2009, p. 14). Notably, this policy led to some targeted youth work being funded from the proceeds of crime (2009, p. 24) as a means of facilitating an alternative response.

Similarly, the continued development of Curriculum for Excellence (CfE) (Education Scotland, 2012) has brought wide-ranging changes in education policy. In relation to youth work, Bridging the Gap: Youth Work and Schools Report (Learning and Teaching Scotland, 2010) highlighted the need for schools to work with other learning providers, such as youth work, in order to enhance young people's life chances. Commenting on this, the Scottish Minister for Skills and Schools (Brown, 2010) acknowledged the importance of youth work in supporting young people and easing their transitions beyond school, while also contributing to their development in relation to the four capacities of CfE: to become confident individuals, responsible citizens, effective contributors and successful learners.

Thus, in some areas of policy development, in Scotland at least, there appears to have been a shift in thinking away from a deficits model and toward more positive approaches to youth work within a more positive environment for policy development. Yet, while the language is often positive, young people remain in a deficient position. For example, in CfE it appears that all young people are assumed as not having assets that mean they are already confident, responsible, contributing effectively and learning well. It is assumed they are deficient in these areas and that a young person centred curriculum will address this deficiency.

Another key policy concerning young people, Getting it Right for Every Child (GIRFEC) (Scottish Government, 2011) is also underpinned by an assumption that as young people progress through their transitions to adulthood, they may face short-term or more complex difficulties and that, regardless of their circumstances, they should be able to access the support and help they need to succeed. Yet, while GIRFEC is suggested as putting the young person at the centre, it is also grounded in a Children's Charter (Scottish Executive, 2004) which pledged support from a range of professional agencies involved in protecting children who are at risk of abuse or neglect. Thus, GIRFEC is similarly focussed on those agencies. So, in addition to values and principles about promoting young people's well-being by building strengths and resilience and by keeping them safe, GIRFEC lists its values and principles as:

> ... legislation, standards, procedures and professional expertise ... respecting confidentiality and sharing information ... promoting the same values across all working relationships ... bringing together each worker's expertise ... co-ordinating help ... building a competent workforce.
>
> Scottish Government (2011, p. 7)

While the policy is overtly about facilitating young people's well-being, some of GIRFECs core values and principles appear to be about 'getting it right' for each of the partner agencies. This could be argued as oppositional to aspirations for putting the child (or young person) at the centre. It also raises questions about what happens with those young people who are not known to those services or partners and have not been identified as in need of professional help. Under GIRFEC, the Scottish Government wanted to introduce a named person for all children from birth to eighteen years old. This person was suggested to be a professional such as a teacher or a health visitor who would be responsible for helping and supporting parents. Although suggested as creating a broader supportive network, the introduction of the scheme was delayed when a Supreme Court ruling found that the proposals 'around information sharing breached the right to privacy and a family life under the European Convention on Human Rights' (BBC, 2016). Those in opposition to the proposals argue that it blurs the boundaries of private and public knowledge, potentially undermines parents and may stretch resources given it would apply to all children not only those in need of additional support (NO2NP, 2017).

Clearly, such policies are intended as a means of socialising young people out of trouble and into successful futures, enabling them to access an appropriate level of support in order to achieve their full potential. Each of these policies offer a useful response to some young people's needs, and are helpful in ensuring targeted support where it is needed most. However, when developed as part of a youth work function, as happens in parts of the United Kingdom, they represent a form of youth work that seeks to control young people or facilitate their socialisation into dominant discourse. This creates conformity to a particular ideology, instead of developing young people's freedom to express their views and take control of their own interests.

Bessant (2007) has already shown that it is difficult for governments to ensure that human rights are consistently upheld in relation to young people and it appears that the capacity to bring about the level of social change required in order for young people to assert their rights may also be limited. Thus, while policy can be an important driver of practice and bring additional funding to support youth and community development, we remain convinced that the policy arena can also force compliance and work against different interests and this is not the main focus for achieving the kind of community action that is required for the level of social change that is needed to challenge inequality.

Yet, in Scotland over the last decade, the move to an outcomes based approach to public sector accountability offers some hope for a different way of thinking with the introduction of a new 'Concordat' (Scottish Government, 2007) and *National Performance Framework* (Scottish Government, 2016). Despite operating within neo-liberal contexts, this framework uses what is called a 'logic model' as a tool in linking activities with outcomes. Logic models have been suggested as having three main uses: policy development, tracking progress and communicating pathways to outcomes.

Outcomes within logic models are time sequenced. The rationale behind the logic model is that if short-term outcomes are achieved this will lead to intermediate and then long-term outcomes being realised. The logic model seeks 'to show how the intervention is expected to work or make a difference ... as part of an iterative approach to building the logic and evidence for claiming that the intervention made a contribution' (Mayne, 2012, p. 271).

However, what was planned and what actually happens may be quite different. Illogical or unexpected events can redefine needs and aspirations. This means that delivering on outcomes does not guarantee a particular output, thus, as a specific measure or predictor of the future, the logic model is flawed. However, used to claim contribution, among a range of other factors that contribute to bringing about change, the logic model is gaining credence among public sector agencies:

> ... using logical arguments to assess the extent to which an intervention was a contributory cause to observed changes ... by "demonstrating contribution" rather than "proving causality" ... while also recognising the limits of their influence and the unpredictability of the external environment.
>
> Wimbush, Montague and Mulherin (2012, p. 312)

Thus, the logic model could be a step in the right direction, in that it offers an understanding that there is a possible link between what is done now and the longer term, future benefits of that activity. The logic model legitimises claims that small-scale outcomes which can be demonstrated might bring a longer-term benefit in future. In Scotland, this model has been used to measure and evaluate the Scottish Alcohol Strategy, which according to Wimbush et al. (2012) means that, these findings have underpinned the introduction of minimum unit pricing and have mapped future plans in order to change 'affordability, availability, knowledge and attitudes' (p. 317). The logic model is being taken seriously at national level in relation to public health. Therefore, it could also be useful in thinking about the contribution of youth work to developing equality.

Yet, while there appears to be an expansion in policies about young people or youth work services, as we have already noted, these tend to be about addressing deficits or perceived problems in young people's lives and are largely developed or more accurately 'delivered' as part of integrated children's services, social work and social welfare services. This kind of work with young people is different from the kind of generic youth work that is educational, cultural and political, where the young person is the primary client and their freedom and emancipation is the core purpose.

In the United Kingdom, the benchmark statements for qualifying programmes in youth work offer guidance on what practitioners are expected to do in those areas where a duality exists, which include:

- Formulating action in association with young people and communities that promotes participation, inclusion, learning and human flourishing;
- Locating and distinguishing practice in the context of inter-professional and multi-disciplinary practice;
- Identifying contemporary debates, key concepts and contested issues within the discipline and comment on them;
- Recognising social theory, social policy and media discourses and their impact on young people and communities.

Adapted from Quality Assurance Agency (2017)
Benchmark Statements for Youth and Community Work

In translating these statements into policy and practice, until there is an extended body of research on the kind of community and youth work that exists in the United Kingdom, we cannot know whether these benchmarks are 'enacted' or whether some elements are lost or misinterpreted. For example, in Scotland there is one national youth work strategy which seeks to work in partnership with young people to create 'a learning process which contributes to improving their life chances, through learning, personal development and active citizenship. Ultimately, we are building stronger, more resilient and inclusive communities' (YouthLink, Education Scotland, 2014, p. 5).

This national strategy suggests that youth work has a major part to play in providing life-enhancing experiences for children and young people. It also illustrates how youth work can engage young people in positive outcomes and articulates a commitment to youth work which is grounded in knowledge and understanding that:

… effective engagement with young people is an empowering process. It offers young people developmental opportunities as well as the ability to lead, take responsibility, make decisions, and make a real and lasting contribution.

YouthLink, Education Scotland (2014, p. 8)

In articulating its ambitions for young people the strategy asserts a belief and commitment to ensuring the contribution of young people as part of their wider communities.

This theme of ambition is articulated in the strategy for adult learning in Scotland, which utilises core principles for learning as lifelong, life-wide, and learner centred, in order to ensure that, 'Scotland becomes recognised globally as the most creative and engaged learning society … [where] … the outcomes that learners achieve will be world-leading' (Education Scotland, 2014, p. 6). While each of these 'statements of ambition' are useful in providing a focus for local activity, they are each couched, in parts, within contemporary trappings of a market driven economy and the compulsion to place particular value on measurable outputs and impacts. Thus, while both are intended as empowering and emancipatory, the lack of critical questioning of the circumstances in which they are written leaves room for misinterpretation and a future for CYW that is neither assured nor clear. We are hopeful that this book offers a critical and questioning edge to conversations about the implementation and development of such statements of ambition. Our aim is to inspire readers to engage in critical dialogue for social change practices that transcend the confines of government or strategically driven policy and practice. In seeking to create authentic community-led statements of ambition that are not as closely aligned to the neoliberal project as current policies, people require to act in order to challenge oppression and so offer hope for an alternative future based on moral and social purposes for democracy and freedom.

Chapter Breakdown

Each chapter within the remainder of this book will address key areas of theory, policy and practice in striving for social change through community and youth work. Chapter 2 articulates the underpinning principles and values that drive an emancipatory practice for social justice and the eradication of inequality. This chapter addresses what we have termed 'hidden knowns', areas that practitioners often discuss as important but which are not presented as routinely as other practice methodologies. In addition, Chapter 2 utilises the work of Wenger (1998), in exploring community and youth work (CYW) as a community of practice (CoP) and suggests ways of extending our current conception of practice.

Chapter 3 explores the key concepts of social justice and equality, articulating the similarities and differences within theory and practice. It moves away from an individualistic focus of society and rather advocates for imaginative practice in problematising our current context while striving for new and alternative discourse that aims for a more socially just and equal world. Chapter 4 adds to this discussion by questioning what we mean by community. It challenges our preconceptions about community engagement and utilises bricolage as a means to frame a variety of constructions of community as a system for connectedness and cohesion. This chapter advocates for a fluid conception of community in order that it can be used as a catalyst for social change.

Chapter 5 analyses the power dimensions throughout communities. It explores how power is often deemed to be a negative tool used to dominate and suppress others. However, this chapter contends that power can be viewed as having agency and capacity to act through activism. It argues for the need to be aware of the fluidity of power whilst being mindful of tokenistic power relations in practice. Chapter 6 discusses the need for practitioners to be critically reflexive and engage in consciousness-raising in order to strive for social change. It analyses the differences between reflection and reflexivity concluding the need for 'emancipatory reflexive praxis' (Taylor, 2010) in generating a strong theoretical underpinning that informs practice towards social change.

Having provided the core concepts and key drivers of emancipatory practice, Chapter 7 begins to explore the practicalities of striving for a more just society within a practice context where the work generally takes place under a patriarchal, neo-liberal, capitalist agenda which individualises and marketises people and places through materialist and divisive processes. This chapter asserts that this creates conditions for us to envision an alternative society and challenges us to think about why we engage in emancipatory practice, how it can help and what sort of society do we want to live in?

Chapter 8 draws on positive psychology to explore how individuals build the capacity to work towards the society they want. It recognises the struggle faced when working within a society that continuously marginalises and vilifies the most vulnerable, and emphasises the wellbeing of self and others in our practice.

Chapter 9 concludes the book by utilising border pedagogy as a threshold concept (Land et al., 2005) in conceptualising CYW as emancipatory praxis. It utilises the theoretical underpinning of critical pedagogy to assert the importance of education as a means of producing identities that are constructed in response to different forms of knowledge and power.

Conclusion

In introducing historical and contemporary contexts for this book, we align with those who assert a value base for equality and democratic purpose in youth work literature (Williamson, 2008; Harland and Morgan, 2006; Scottish Government, 2007). However, changes in the policy environment have led to increased use of informal youth work methods in a range of contexts, such as jobs access activity or health improvement. While these policy developments are needed and welcomed, the resultant shift in youth work practice has led to creation of a more outcome and output driven practice. There is a consensus in youth work literature that aspects of this policy shift appears to contradict the founding principles of youth work and its distinctive social and democratic purpose (Davies, 2005; Jeffs and Smith, 2010; Wallace, 2008). Our aim in writing this book is to assert community youth work as an emancipatory practice. This chapter has outlined the neoliberal conditions that underpin theoretical and political contexts for CYW practice, in the United Kingdom and elsewhere. In order to achieve this aim, the next chapter considers core values and principles that underpin the development of practice and thereafter, core ideas from theory, policy and practice are discussed in order to assist readers to engage in practice for equality social justice.

Bibliography

Aronowitz, S. (2009). Against schooling: Education and social class. In A. Darder, M. Baltodano and R. Torres (Eds.), *The Critical Pedagogy Reader* (pp. 106–122). Oxon: Routledge.

Baker, J., Lynch, K., Cantillion, S. and Walsh, J. (2004). *Equality: From Theory to Action.* Basingstoke: Palgrave Macmillan.

Baker, J., Lynch, K., Cantillion, S. and Walsh, J. (2009). *Equality: From Theory to Action: Second Edition.* Basingstoke: Palgrave Macmillan.

Banks, S. (2010). *Ethical Issues in Youth Work.* London: Routledge.

Barber, T. (2007). Who is youth work for? Distortions and possibilities. *Scottish Youth Issues Journal, 9,* 77–88.

Batsleer, J. (2008). *Informal Learning in Youth Work*. London: Sage.

Batsleer, J. and Davies B. (Eds.) (2010). *What is Youth Work?* (pp. 140–152). Exeter: Learning Matters.

Beatty, C., Foden, M., McCarthy, L. and Reeve, K. (2015). *Benefit Sanctions and Homelessness: A Scoping Report*. London: Crisis.

Beatty, C and Fothergill, S. (2013). *Hitting the Poorest Places Hardest: The local and regional impact of welfare reform*, Centre for Regional Economic and Social Research: Sheffield Hallam University.

BBC. (2016). *What is the named person scheme?* Accessed 10th February 2016 at http://www.bbc.co.uk/news/ukscotland-scotland-politics-35752756

Beierling, S. (2014). A fat woman's story of body-image, politics and the weighty discourses of magnification and minimization. In S. Steinberg and A. Ibrahim, *Critical Youth Studies Reader*. New York: Peter Lang.

Bessant, J. (2007). Not such a fair go: An audit of children's and young people's rights in Australia. *Scottish Youth Issues Journal*, 9, 41–56. Accessed 15th February 2008 from http://www.youthlinkscotland.org/webs/245/documents/SYIJIss9.pdf

Brown, K. (2010). Bridging the Gap. Accessed 13 February 2012 at: http://www.educationscotland.gov.uk/connected/b/genericcontent_tcm4564142.asp

Coburn, A. (2011). Liberation or containment: Paradoxes in youth work as a catalyst for powerful learning. *Journal of Youth and Policy* (106). 66–77.

Coburn, A. (2012). Learning about equality: A study of a generic youth work setting. PhD thesis, University of Strathclyde. Accessed on 30 September 2016 at http://suprimo.lib.strath.ac.uk/primo_library/libweb/action/search.do

Coburn, A. and McCafferty, P. (2016). The *real* Olympics games: Sponsorship, schools and the Olympics – The case of Coca Cola. *Taboo: the Journal of Culture and Education* 15(1), 23–40. Retrieved 14 May from http://www.freireproject.org/download/journals/taboo/06coburnmccafferty.pdf

Coburn, A. and Gormally, S. (2015). Emancipatory praxis: A social-justice approach to equality work. In C. Cooper, S. Gormally, and G. Hughes (Eds.), *Socially-Just, Radical Alternatives for Education and Youth Work Practice: Re-Imagining Ways of Working with Young People*. Basingstoke: Palgrave MacMillan.

Coburn, A. and Gormally, S. (2015a). Youth work in schools. In G. Bright, *Youth Work: Histories, Policy and Contexts*. London: Palgrave.

Coburn, A. and Wallace, D. (2011). *Youth Work in Communities and Schools*. Edinburgh: Dunedin Press.

Cohen, P. (1997). *Rethinking the Youth Question: Education, Labour and Cultural Studies*. Basingstoke: Macmillan.

Darder A., Baltodano, M. and Torres, R. (Eds) (2009). *The Critical Pedagogy Reader*. Oxon: Routledge.

Davies, B. (2005). Youth work: A manifesto for our times. *Journal of Youth and Policy*, 88, 1–23.

Davies, B. (2011). 'What's positive for youth? A critical look at the Government's emerging "youth policy"', *Youth & Policy* pp. 107: 99–104.

Davies, B. (2015). Youth work: A manifesto for our times—Revisited. *Journal of Youth and Policy*, 114, 96–117.

Davies, B. and Merton, B. (2009). *Squaring the Circle: Findings of a 'Modest Inquiry' into the State of Youth Work Practice in a Changing Policy Environment*. Leicester: University of DeMontfort.

De Corte, E., Versgaffel, L., Entwistle, N. and Van Merrienboer, J. (2003). *Powerful Learning Environments: Unraveling Basic Components and Dimensions*. London: Pergamon.

De St Croix, T. (2010). Youth work and the surveillance state. In J. Batsleer and B. Davies (Eds.), *What Is Youth Work?* (pp. 140–152). Exeter: Learning Matters.

Education Scotland (2014). *Adult learning in Scotland: Statement of ambition*. Accessed on 20 September 2016 at http://www.educationscotland.gov.uk/Images/AdultLearningStatemento-fAmbition_tcm4-826940.pdf

Education Scotland/YouthLink. (2014). Our ambitions for improving the life chances of young people in Scotland. Accessed on 20 September 2016 at http://www.educationscotland.gov.uk/Images/YouthWorkStrategy181214_tcm4-823155.pdf

Education Scotland. (2012). What is curriculum for excellence? Retrieved 6 January 2012 from http://www.educationscotland.gov.uk/thecurriculum/whatiscurriculumforexcellence/index.asp

European Commission. (2001). A new impetus for youth. White Paper. Retrieved 25 February 2016 from http://ec.europa.eu/youth/documents/publications/whitepaper_en.pdf

European Union. (2006). Youth forum manifesto: From diversity to equality, the missing link. Retrieved 12 January 2016 from http://youthforum.org/fr/system/files/yfj_public/strategic_priorities/en/0600-06Manifesto_FINAL.pdf

Epstein, R. (2007). *The Case Against Adolescence: Rediscovering the Adult in Every Teen*. Sanger, California: Quill Driver Books.

Freire, P. (1996). *Pedagogy of the Oppressed* (M. B. Ramos, Trans. 2nd Ed.). London: Penguin.

Furlong, A. and Cartmel, F. (2007). *Young People and Social Change: Individualisation and Risk in Late Modernity*. Buckingham: Open University Press.

Fyffe, I. (2010) Young people and community engagement. In L. Tett, *Community Learning and Development* (3rd Ed.). Edinburgh: Dunedin Academic Press.

Giddens, A. (2003). *Sociology* (4th Ed.). Cambridge: Polity Press.

Giroux, H. (2012). *Education and the Crisis of Public Values: Challenging the Assault on Teachers, Students and Public Education*. New York: Peter Lang.

Giroux, H. (2009) *Youth in a Suspect Society*. Basingstoke: Palgrave MacMillan.

Giroux, H. (2005). *Border Crossings*. Oxon: Routledge.

Gormally, S. and Deuchar, R. (2012) Somewhere between distrust and dependence: Young people, the police and anti-social behaviour management within marginalised communities. *The International Journal on School Disaffection*. 9(1), 51–66.

Gormally, S. (2015). 'I've been there, done that ...': A study of youth gang desistance, *Youth Justice*, 15(2), 148–165.

Green, L. (2010). *Understanding the Life Course: Sociological and Psychological perspectives*. Cambridge: Polity.

Griggs, J. and Evans, M. (2010). *Sanctions Within Conditional Benefit Systems: A Review of Evidence*. York: Joseph Rowntree Foundation.

Hallsworth, S. and Young, T. (2008). Gang talk and gang talkers: A critique. *Crime, Media, Culture: An International Journal*, 4(2), 175–195.

Harland, K. and Morgan, T. (2006). Youth work in Northern Ireland: An exploration of emerging themes and challenges. *Youth Studies Ireland*, 1(1), 4–18.

Harland, K. and McCready, S. (2012) Taking boys seriously—A longitudinal study of adolescent male school-life experiences in Northern Ireland. Jordanstown, University of Ulster, Department of Justice of Northern Ireland.

Harland, K., Harvey, C., Morgan, T. and McCready, S. (2005). Worth their weight in gold: The views of community youth work graduates in Northern Ireland in their chosen career. *Journal of Youth and Policy*, 86, 49–61.

Jeffs, T. and Banks, S. (2010). Youth workers as controllers: Issues of method and purpose. In S. Banks (Ed.), *Ethical Issues in Youth Work* (pp. 106–123). London: Routledge.

Jeffs, T. and Smith, M. K. (Eds.) (2010). *Youth Work Practice*. Basingstoke: Palgrave Macmillan.

Jeffs, T. and Smith, M. K. (2005). *Informal Education, Conversation, Democracy and Learning* (3rd Ed.). Derby: Education Now.

Jeffs, T. and Smith, M. K. (1999). The problem of youth for youth work. *Journal of Youth and Policy*, 62, 45–66.

Jones, G. and Bell, R. (2000). *Balancing Acts: Youth, Parenting and Public Policy*. York: Joseph Rowntree Foundation.

Kincheloe, J. (2008). *Critical Pedagogy*. New York: Peter Lang.

Konings, K., Brand-Gruwel, S. and van Merrienboer, J. (2005). Towards more powerful learning environments through combining the perspectives of designers, teachers and students. *British Journal of Educational Psychology*, 75, 645–660.

Lave, J. and Wenger, E. (1991). *Situated Learning: Legitimate Peripheral Participation*. Cambridge: Cambridge University Press.

Learning and Teaching Scotland (2010). Bridging the Gap: Improving Outcomes for Scotland's Young People through School and Youth Work Partnerships, Accessed on 12 May 2017 at http://www.youthscotland.org.uk/publications/youth-scotland-resources/publications.htm

Lifelong Learning UK (LLUK) (2008). *National occupational standards for youth work*. Accessed on 10 October 2015 at http://webarchive.nationalarchives.gov.uk/20110414152025/http:/www.lluk.org/wp-content/uploads/2010/11/National-Occupational-Standards-for-Youth-Work.pdf

Mayne, J. (2012). Contribution Analysis: Coming of Age? *Evaluation*, 18, 270–295.

MacAlister-Brew, J. (1943). *In the Service of Youth*. London: Faber and Faber.

McCulloch, K. (2007). Democratic participation or surveillance? Structures and practices for young people's decision-making. *Scottish Youth Issues Journal*, 9, 9–22.

MacDonald, R. and Marsh, J. (2005). *Disconnected Youth? Growing Up in Poor Britain*. Basingstoke: Palgrave.

McIntyre, J. (2014). 'Right I can do this now': Community based adult learning, health and well-being. Concept: *The Journal of Contemporary Community Education Practice and Theory*, 5(3), pp. 12–20.

Martin, I. (2001). Lifelong learning: For earning, yawning or yearning. *Adults Learning*, *13*(2), 14–17.

Martin, I. (2007). Reclaiming social purpose: Framing the discussion. *The Edinburgh Papers*. Edinburgh: Edinburgh University.

Milburn, R., Clark, J., Forde, L., Fulton, K., Locke, A. and MacQuarrie, E. (1995). *Curriculum Development in Youth Work*. Edinburgh: SOED.

Mizen, P. (2004). *The Changing State of Youth*. Basingstoke: Palgrave MacMillan.

Morgan, T. and O'Hare, B. (2001). The excluded adolescent: An exploration of the issues surrounding marginalised young people in Northern Ireland. *Scottish Youth Issues Journal*, *3*, 49–68.

NO2NP. (2017). *No to Named Person Scheme*. Accessed on 10th February 2017 at http://no2np. org/named-person/

O'Donnell, M. (1997). *Sociology: An Introduction*. Walton-on-Thames: Nelson.

Oakley, M. (2014). Independent review of the operation of Jobseeker's Allowance Sanctions validated by the Jobseekers Act 2013. London: JSA Sanctions Independent Review Team.

Quality Assurance Agency for Higher Education. (2017). *Subject benchmark statement: Youth and community work*. Retrieved 4 May 2017 at http://www.qaa.ac.uk/en/Publications/Documents/SBS-Youth-and-Community-Work-17.pdf

Roberts, S. (2011). Beyond 'NEET' and 'tidy' pathways: Considering the 'missing middle' of youth transition studies. *Journal of Youth Studies*, *14*(1), 21–39.

Robertson, S (2005). *Youth Clubs: Association, Participation, Friendship and Fun*, Lyme Regis: Russell House Publishing.

Scottish Education Department (1975). *Adult education: the challenge of change. Report by a Committee of Inquiry* (The Alexander Report). Edinburgh: HMSO.

Sercombe, H. (2010). *Youth Work Ethics*. London: Sage.

Scottish Government. (2016). National Performance Framework. Accessed 3 March 2016 at http://www.gov.scot/About/Performance/scotPerforms/pdfNPF

Scottish Government. (2011). *Getting it right for every child Scotland (GIRFEC)*. Retrieved 30 May 2014 from http://www.scotland.gov.uk/Topics/People/Young-People/gettingitright

Scottish Government. (2011a). *Promoting positive outcomes: Working together to prevent anti-social behaviour in Scotland*. Retrieved 30 May 2011 from http://www.scotland.gov.uk/ Publications/2009/03/18112243/16

Scottish Government. (2009). *Promoting positive outcomes: Working together to prevent anti-social behaviour in Scotland*. Retrieved May 30, 2014, from http://www.scotland.gov.uk/ Publications/2009/03/18112243/0

Scottish Government. (2007). Concordat between the Scottish government and local government. Accessed on 7 March 2016 at http://www.gov.scot/Resource/Doc/923/0054147.pdf

Scottish Youth Parliament. (2016). About SYP. Accessed on 12 January at http://www.syp.org. uk/about_syp

Sen, A. (1985).Well-being, agency and freedom: The Dewey lectures 1984. *Journal of Philosophy* *82*, 169–221. Retrieved 10 May 2016 from http://www.freelogy.org/w/images/d/dc/Sen85.pdf

Shaw, M. (2008). Policy, Politics and Practice: Community Development. *The Edinburgh papers: Reclaimining Social Purpose in Community Education*. Edinburgh: Reclaiming Social Purpose

Group. Retrieved 1st Oct 2013 at, http://criticallychatting.files.wordpress.com/2008/11/theedinburghpapers-pdf.pdf

Shaw, M. and McCulloch, K. (2009). Hooligans or rebels? Thinking more critically about citizenship and young people. *Journal of Youth and Policy*, No. 101, pp. 5–14.

Smyth, J. (2014). An 'evolving criticality' in youth and/or student voice in schools in hardening neoliberal times. In S. Steinberg and A. Ibrahim, *Critical Youth Studies Reader*. New York: Peter Lang.

Steinberg, S. (2011). *Kinderculture: The Corporate Construction of Childhood*. (3rd Ed.) Boulder, Colorado: Westview Press.

Strathclyde Regional Council. (1984). *Working with Young People*. Glasgow: SRC.

Taylor, T. (2008). Young people, politics and participation: A youth work perspective. *Journal of Youth and Policy*, 100, 253–263.

Taylor, T. (2010). Defending democratic youth work. *Concept, 1*(2), 3–10.

Tett, L. (2006). *Community Learning and Development* (2nd Ed.). Edinburgh: Dunedin Academic Press.

Tett, L. (2010). *Community Learning and Development* (3rd Ed.). Edinburgh: Dunedin Academic Press.

Thorp, A. and Kennedy, S. (2010). The problems of British society: Is Britain broken? What are the policy implications? Accessed on 10 October 2015 from http://www.parliament.uk/documents/commons/lib/research/key_issues/Key-Issues-The-problems-of-British-society.pdf

United Nations. (1989). *United Nations Convention on the Rights of the Child* (UNCROC). Adopted by the General Assembly of the United Nations, 20th November, 2014.

Waiton, S. (2001). *Scared of the Kids? Curfews, Crime and the Regulation of Young People*. Sheffield: Sheffield Hallam University Press.

Wallace, D. (2008). Community education and community learning and development (post devolution). In T. Bryce and W. Humes, *Scottish Education (3rd Ed.), Beyond Devolution*. Edinburgh: Edinburgh University Press.

Wenger, E. (1998). *Communities of Practice: Learning, Meaning and Identity*. Cambridge: Cambridge University Press.

Wenger, E. and Traynor, B. (2015). Communities of practice: A brief introduction. Available at http://wenger-trayner.com/wp-content/uploads/2015/04/07-Brief-introduction-to-communities-of-practice.pdf

Williamson, H. (2008). European Youth Policy, *Youth & Policy*, No. 100, Summer/Autumn 2008.

Wimbush, E., Montague, S. and Mulherin, T. (2012). Applications of contribution analysis to outcome planning and impact evaluation. *Evaluation*, 18, 310–329.

Wyn, J. and White, R. (1997). *Rethinking Youth*. London: Sage.

YouthLink, Education Scotland (2014). Our ambitions for improving the life chances of young people in Scotland National Youth Work Strategy 2014–2019, Accessed on 20 April 2016 at http://www.south-ayrshire.gov.uk/documents/nationalyouthworkstrategy.pdf

Young, K. (2006). *The Art of Youth Work* (2nd Ed.). Lyme Regis: Russell House Publishing.

· 2 ·

STRIVING FOR UNIFYING
PRINCIPLES AND VALUES

Introduction

This chapter is driven by our wider concerns that community and youth work (CYW) practice is increasingly focussed on what and how we do things, as distinct from articulating and enacting the underpinning principles and values that drive an emancipatory practice for social justice and the eradication of inequality (Coburn and Gormally, 2015). We are puzzled by what we have termed the 'hidden knowns' of youth and community practices (Coburn and Gormally, 2014). As a work in progress, we are interested in a range of 'hidden knowns' that practitioners know are important in practice but which are rarely evaluated and discussed to the same depth or level of detail as more routine practice methodologies. Yet, we believe these 'hidden knowns' are core elements of educational CYW practice that make a definitional contribution to minimise any confusion in comparison with professions such as social work or school teaching.

This chapter considers core aspects of practice and raises questions on their potential contribution to strengthening a Community of Practice (CoP) (Lave and Wenger, 1991; Wenger and Traynor, 2015) for equality work within CYW contexts in order to achieve a more equitable society.

We then describe what we mean by 'hidden knowns' as distinctive aspects of practice that add to knowledge and understanding of how youth and community work can reclaim and assert its emancipatory purpose. Finally, aligned to the idea of principles and values that inform consideration of professional identity amidst a diversification of practice, we reassert youth and community worker identity as purposeful and deliberate in striving for emancipatory social change.

The connection between identity and a community of practice is foundational to the experience of becoming a practitioner, 'of being a person in that context' (Wenger, 1998 p. 149). Wenger identified five characterisations of identity as:

- Identity as *negotiated experience*. We define who we are by the ways we experience ourselves through participation as well as by the ways we and others reify our selves
- Identity as *community membership*. We define who we are by the familiar and the unfamiliar.
- Identity as *learning trajectory*. We define who we are by where we have been and where we are going.
- Identity as *nexus of multi-membership*. We define who we are by the ways we reconcile our various forms of membership into one identity.
- Identity as a *relation between the local and the global*. We define who we are by negotiating local ways of belonging to broader constellations and of manifesting broader styles ad discourses.

Wenger (1998, p. 149)

Discussion is developed within the context of an emerging community of practice in youth and community work which, according to Wenger (1998), involves both community participation by practitioners involved in the practice area, and also the development of artefacts, models and curricula that can be used to convince others of the veracity of the practice undertaken in the professional community. We propose that such discussion of practice, and in particular the 'hidden knowns' of practice, can unify and extend possibilities for thinking beyond current professional disciplines, to invigorate regional, national and international praxis and contribute to the development and definition of an emerging CoP, in community and youth work.

Community and Youth Work Practice ...
Where Are We Now?

In times of economic recession and a referendum fuelled political 'enlightenment', it is useful to reflect on aspects of practice that shape our world view and help us to define our professional identity in order to consider who we are and how we are defined, and so create distinction from other practices. The emergence of social movements that occupy public spaces have revitalised public protest about social inequality and, closer to home, the In Defence of Youth Work campaign has become a catalyst for sustained dialogue on the nature and purpose of particular kinds of professional practice and the cornerstones of youth work. Both are testament to the capacity of people to act together in human endeavour in order to facilitate the creation of an alternative worldview that seeks new ways of being in the world.

This is an interesting and challenging period in youth and community work history. A grinding down of the public sector through persistent restructuring, reinvention, or disinvestment in youth and community work services, by those who misinterpret practice as variously behaviour management or careers guidance, suggests some urgency in needing to rethink or reassert alternative forms of practice. In this sense, we align with authors who also propose youth and community work as a critical practice that is configured as social and educational endeavour with an emancipatory democratic purpose (Coburn and Wallace, 2011; Davies, 2005; 2015; Jeffs and Smith, 2005; 2010; Ledwith, 2007; Ledwith, 2016; Martin, 2007; Shaw and McCulloch, 2009; Taylor, 2008; 2010).

Having a dual inclination towards both sustaining and developing current practices, including those that take a critical stance in challenging the status quo, and those that are consistent with prevailing social policy agendas, can offer possibilities for radical community development methods to be introduced (Coburn and Gormally, 2015). This dual inclination facilitates praxis by starting not only where people in communities are starting, but also where policy is emerging, in order to facilitate work with people that enables them to develop the kind of attributes, capabilities and strengths that will help them to make a good life (Sen, 1985). It also enables a critical analysis of power relations and the neo-liberal project, in mitigation of formulaic short termism and individualistic materialism. For example, in critical youth work (Coburn and Wallace, 2011; Coburn and Gormally, 2015) the response to youth unem-ployment facilitates functionality in basic skills development, and creates a more emancipatory and critical practice in consciously challenging the status quo on why young people are unemployed and what can be done to change or improve this situation.

Rather than taking a position of compliance, CYW rejects generalised acceptance of a capitalist status quo and seeks to re-imagine and to think beyond existing knowledge in order to work with people to create a more socially just society, where:

> Community development practice needs to develop strategies that challenge this consciousness and balance the needs of business against the needs of local communities.
>
> Ledwith (2011, p. 170)

As a professional CoP, not yet clearly defined or recognised as such, we need to 'do' the practice to make it visible and to be articulated as import-ant to people outside of our immediate experience—including politicians, different professional, disciplinary areas or wider community members. In combining informal educational processes with an explicit emancipatory purpose, we can enhance focus on process and purpose, which is driven by communities we work with, rather than having content scheduled or measurable products determined by funders or others, who claim to know what's best for communities and people. Although this has always been the focus in youth and community praxis, this emancipatory purpose appears often as an understated aspect of CYW practice, routinely hidden from the view of participants or funders, but cited by practitioners as a core ratio-nale for practice. An emancipatory purpose for CYW can thus be suggested as a 'hidden known' among practitioners who articulate social justice and equality as their main focus, but who are routinely and often unconsciously complicit in maintaining the status quo. The reification and visibility of practice (see Chapter 4) remains problematic and it is for this reason that we seek to identify and bring forward discussion of 'hidden knowns' as an important aspect for consideration within a distinctive community of practice.

The next section offers a number of unifying values and practice princi-ples which can contribute to the development of a professional community of practice around which to plan and to negotiate, 'local ways of belonging to broader constellations' (Wenger, 1998, p. 149).

'Hidden Knowns'

One way of unifying practitioner identity is through making the 'hidden knowns' visible. In a previous exploratory article (Gormally and Coburn, 2014), we identified five elements where youth work practice aligned with research processes: reflexivity; positionality and bias; insider cultural competence; rapport and trust, and power relationships. Subsequently, we have presented these at an academic conference as some of the 'hidden knowns' of youth work and community development practice (Coburn and Gormally, 2014). These practices are further examined here to show that, as practitioners and academics, we 'know' they exist and are important but often we take them for granted and do not always convey them effectively or explicitly to others. This makes them somewhat 'hidden' from those who need to know about them in order to understand and to reinforce that youth work and community development are vitally important practices. We suggest that these 'hidden knowns' underpin what university courses teach, what we 'do' in the field professionally and what we see as our common thread that binds us together as a particular Community of Practice. In this sense, the 'hidden knowns' can inform what is described by Wenger and Traynor (2015) as a Domain of Practice:

> an identity defined by a shared domain of interest ... Membership therefore implies a commitment to the domain, and therefore a shared competence that distinguishes members from other people ... The domain is not necessarily something recognized as "expertise" outside the community.

Conversely, practitioners sometimes specifically choose to adopt 'hidden' practices. They take a back seat, in order to promote others' voice and hide from the limelight. We are not suggesting this as problematic but what we do assert here is that what we do, and how we do it, needs to be made visible and explicit to clearly demonstrate our underpinning rationale for why we practice in particular ways. Making practices visible, assists in avoiding mistakes in future and helps in ensuring that our practices are known as carefully developed over time, rather than being assumed as having no foundational principles, values and practices.

As we will explore later the importance of reflexivity and of our own positionality or bias, underpins practice that starts where people are (Davies, 2005), in analysing power relations. However, where these 'hidden knowns' are not articulated effectively, they have become a hegemonic normality in our practice domain. This suggests a need to articulate such practices more effectively, to reify practice in ways that highlight the benefits produced, whilst fundamentally reasserting that these practices aid our commitment to social justice and equality. The rest of this chapter will provide an overview of the 'hidden knowns' and articulate why we feel that a community and youth work CoP should be reasserted more clearly and our professional identity articulated as emancipatory, in advocating for a more socially just and equitable society.

We Hide Our Explicit Interest in Social Justice and Equality

Our approach to social justice and equality is premised in:

> ... our argument is that theory on social justice and equality are aligned in their agreement that structural disadvantage, discrimination and inequality must be challenged and addressed. This can be done through a twofold approach which analyses the redistribution of economic resources, whilst also acknowledging the importance of recognition.
>
> Coburn and Gormally (2015, p. 70)

We are explicit in our concerns that CYW practice is not articulated clearly enough in terms of an emancipatory struggle for equality. Rather, practice has become increasingly focussed on outcomes, which subscribe to deficit policy models, perpetuated by neoliberalism. If we aspire to create a more equal and fairer democratic society, Baker et al. (2004) suggest a need for radical social change. Resisting a tick-box culture (Batsleer, 2008) could shift focus beyond the scope of an increasingly prescriptive curriculum that is moving closer toward accredited learning as a key driver of policy and practice in youth work and community-based adult learning. Seeing value in enhancing power-sharing possibilities and producing community resilience (see chapter 8) could be key to shifting emphasis away from the individual as deficient and 'needy' and towards a collaborative engagement that is democratic and emancipatory, where people work together with and for each other, to play a full part in developing themselves and their communities.

In the United States, the position of young people is also identified as being, 'removed from the inventory of social concerns and the list of cherished public assets, young people have been either disparaged as a symbol of danger or simply rendered invisible' (Giroux, 2014, p. 101). Within a context of socially constructed age-based and often negative discourse, youth work seeks to meaningfully engage with young people so that they can reclaim their power (Davies, 2005; Young, 2006). This includes a commitment to action where 'power relations shift and are transformed ... [and where] ... a closer analysis of power relationships and their impact on practice, is a prerequisite of the work we undertake' (Batsleer, 2008, p. 9). This is consistent with perspectives on youth work as a process of seeking to challenge and to question where, 'youth workers need to be more political with the rights of young people central to their practice' (Gallagher and Morgan, 2013, p. 43). In this way, youth work is a socio-political endeavour that engages in educational activity with young people so they can determine and be responsible for their lives, now and in future. While informal methods of engagement can include a range of activities such as social, sporting and arts based activities, these in themselves do not facilitate social change, they are simply ways of connecting with people, in order to develop deeper relationships of respect and trust that underpin conversations about power and social justice. Yet, they do offer a starting point for otherwise disengaged people and communities.

Such forms of engagement offer a useful and person-centred alternative to the emergence of formulaic and credit-bearing programmes that community workers are increasingly expected to 'deliver' as a prescription for employability or parenting which are, in themselves, problematic because they reduce education and people to learning commodities that are traded in the marketplace (Giroux, 2009; 2016). Further, the formulaic does not tackle the underpinning assumptions about the conditions in which people are required to become 'more employable' or a 'better parent'. Such programmes target particular people, labelled as NEET (Not in Education, Employment or Training) or vulnerable, in seeking to achieve specific and measureable outcomes that are often driven by current policy or funder interests that seek to 'fix' young people who are identified as marginal or damaged.

This is not the same as open access or generic youth work, which accepts young people as they are and 'to which young people have chosen to come ... [where practice is] ... proactively seeking to tip the balances of power towards young people' (Davies, 2015, p. 100). Open access youth work happens in a range of settings that include dedicated leisure-time or social spaces such as cafés and youth centres. It is also located where young people choose to meet each other socially, such as local parks, during lunch breaks or after formal schooling. This kind of youth work positions the young person as the primary client (Sercombe, 2010) and takes time to build relationships of trust and respect by working across social and cultural boundaries in order to engage with young people who are seen as 'capable social actors ... [where] ... equality and social justice are core concerns' (Coburn and Wallace, 2011, p. 15).

The idea that a meaningful 12-week quick-fix programme exists, in regard to important aspects of young people's lives, is troublesome. This kind of targeted interventionist work, often achieved through imposition of sanctions or rewards/awards, rather than a flexible and negotiated curriculum, does not sit comfortably within youth work's democratic purpose. While basic skills can be learned over short periods and specific moments can be interpreted as important in personal transformation, to suggest that this solely constitutes youth work as a distinct professional area, such as school teaching or careers guidance, falls short of the mark by accommodating rather than challenging the status quo. However, such work can be described as what Coburn and Wallace (2011) identified as 'functional youth work' (p. 13) which promotes individual development that mitigates risk-taking or negative behaviour by promoting positive self-image through improved education.

Such programmes can thus offer a starting point for youth work that engages young people over a prolonged period, to improve their chances of making a good life. These can be integrated into open access provision but are not the same as practice where 'participation in self-chosen "open access" settings as a—perhaps the—defining feature of practice which claims "youth work" as its title' (Davies, 2005; 2015).

In contrast to the persistent neo-liberal discourse, our aspiration is therefore to continue to highlight, defend and rearticulate the social and democratic purpose of youth work, adult education and community development (Buchroth, and Parkin, 2010; Davies, 2005; Jeffs and Smith, 2010; Martin, 2007; Smith, 2002; Taylor, 2010; Tett, 2010; Young, 2006).

We previously developed a model of practice which explores power relations, promotes a critical consciousness-raising at micro and macro levels, and offers a means of reasserting practice as emancipatory (Coburn and Gormally, 2015). Drawing on Ginwright and Cammarota (2002) who developed a social justice approach to youth development, the work of Coburn (2012) on negotiation of relationships within a youth work setting, and Baker et al.'s (2004) five dimensions of equality, we argue that this visual image demonstrates the processes for relationship building that support consciousness raising as an underpinning aspect of effective praxis. These process are not solely cyclical and each stage is important in itself in contributing to emancipatory praxis.

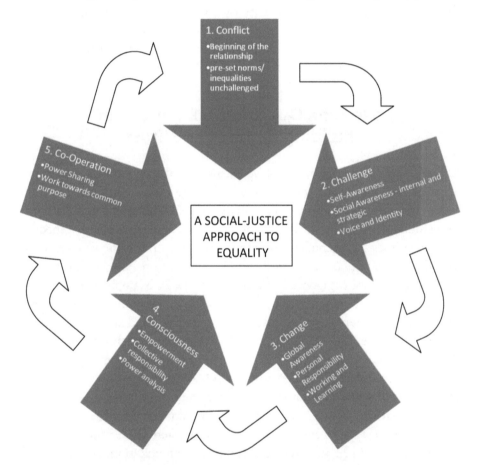

Figure 1. A social justice approach to equality. (Coburn and Gormally, 2015)

There are, however, other models or criteria that have effectively captured CYW practice in terms of what we do and the outcomes we achieve. Creating such models, helps to develop practice, but there is scope for a range of different models to be discussed, as these help to 'reconcile our various forms of membership into one identity' (Wenger, 1998, p. 149). So, while this model is in itself useful, it can also be adapted, interpreted and applied to work across a range of contexts in an effort to understand praxis, and to unpack the professional dilemmas and alternative dispositions required for authentic praxis.

Thus, our model helps in articulating the biggest 'hidden known' of CYW practice—its emancipatory core—where the purpose of our work is (at micro and macro levels) to fundamentally to work with communities to bring about change and enhanced capacity for social justice and equality. Instead of explaining the model, our purpose here is to outline five of the 'hidden knowns' that underpin its development, so that practitioners can begin conversations about known and unknown aspects of professional practice.

We Hide Our Known Expertise in Building Rapport and Trust

As youth and community workers, we are aware of the importance of spending time building rapport and trust in order to develop strong relationships. At the beginning of the relationship rapport helps to break the ice and establish common ground. During the early stages of interaction, pre-set norms and inequalities sometimes go unchallenged. This means that power is assumed to sit with the community or youth worker and language or behaviour that sustains inequality is sometimes ignored, or missed entirely, for example, in use of terms such as, 'leader' or, being 'in charge'. Nevertheless, in working with groups of people who are often identified by others as marginal, and are criminalised or viewed as 'undeserving' (Cooper et al, 2015), we are clear about the necessity of starting where people are starting, in order to develop meaningful and relevant pedagogy. During early encounters, rapport is often needed to facilitate engagement in purposeful conversation that helps us to find out about where people are without being overly intrusive. The notion of trusting in the process, of spending time to ensure that we 'actively listen' (Robertson, 2005) and that we do not engage in tokenistic relations, are foundational to practice. It is 'common knowledge' amongst practitioners that informal conversations in groups or with individuals, around a specific activity or issue, are purposefully used to facilitate dialogue (Spence et al., 2006) and that in a research context:

> Developing trust with young people by taking an interest in them, spending time with them and engaging in conversations beyond the immediate research topic helped build rapport.
>
> Gormally and Coburn (2014, p. 12)

This building of trust and rapport is mutual. As people get to know each other better and become more relaxed in each other's company it is possible to create rapport that helps foster friendly and trusting relationships which, according to Glesne (1989), offers mutual understanding and respect but not necessarily liking each other. It is important that those we work with trust our practices as ethically and morally sound, so that they trust in the process, trust in the uncertainty of building relationships and trust in finding a new journey together which may be difficult. This is especially compelling where the conditions for trust between adults and young people often run counter to a normative hegemonic narrative which sustains opposition and mistrust in communities. In this way, trust and rapport are vital both within oneself and with others, in building our next hidden known—reflexivity.

We Hide Our Known Expertise in Being Reflexive Practitioners

As community and youth workers, we understand the combined efficiencies and requirements for self-awareness, social and spatial awareness, voice and identity. In chapter six, we show how these can be effectively articulated through being reflexive practitioners. Taylor (2010) suggests that emancipatory reflection has a central focus in transformative action and that to achieve emancipatory reflection a process of praxis is required. Reflexivity is not solely focussed on knowledge gathering, it is also used to change our own practice when used as a tool that supports emancipatory practice for social justice (Coburn and Gormally, 2015). Although reflection and reflexivity are 'hidden knowns', as CYW practitioners we should adopt emancipatory reflexive praxis to ensure a sceptical criticality, a deep analysis of power relations and to generate awareness of the theory and practice knowledge which underpins emancipatory processes (see Chapter 6).

We Hide Our Purposeful Engagement in Power Analysis

Power analysis is crucial in reflexive practice and in the negotiation processes that underpin the struggle for a more socially just and equitable world. Analysis of power is acutely important for youth work and community development practitioners, especially in creating conditions for power sharing, and as such is a key 'hidden known'. In Chapter 4, we show that power is not a static object given to one person or another but rather it can be viewed as a capacity that is within all of us. This analysis is often underplayed but community practitioners who are engaged in generating social change. Thus, our role as facilitators of power analysis within communities is less visible than it could be in accepting the level of community and individual influence that we bring to the educational relationship. As noted on research of community activists in Northern Ireland:

> Community activists often dismiss the idea that they exercise power, preferring to speak in terms of influence, but arguably this is to under-estimate the importance of the vibrant collective activity that took place over the years of the Troubles and subsequent period of peace building.
>
> Kilmurray (2017, p. 292)

As a 'hidden known', it is important to consider the extent to which practice impacts on the kinds of change that happens in our work with people and in communities, to show the contribution of community work in facilitating conditions for micro and macro levels of change. The various conditions and levels of power are discussed in more detail in Chapter 5.

We Hide Our Capacities for Building Community Resilience

Resilience seems to be becoming the panacea for practice in numerous sectors. This ranges from 'bouncebackability' in sporting discourse to character building in public policy. We need to be careful not to subscribe to an uncritical 'buy-in' of this particular language and narrative that in essence places blame on the most vulnerable in society. The building of resilience, for example, is seen as a positive attribute where individuals can deal with problems, as distinct from facilitating consciousness to challenge their root cause. Individual resilience is utilised by many professions as a means to understanding how some people 'cope' in certain circumstances whilst other do not. The heralding of 'personal resilience' is evident in recent policies and governmental funding priorities. The UK government has recently opened a call for 'character grants' worth £6 million aimed at schools promoting traits such as resilience and respect. These grants also include up to £2 million earmarked for projects with a military ethos, highlighting the type of character deemed as important. Children and Families Minister Edward Timpson (2016) said:

Instilling positive character traits and academic excellence are 2 sides of the same coin - children that develop resilience are far more likely to succeed, not only in school but in later life, too.

Scottish Government (2016)

In Chapter 8, we discuss the potential for a more collective resilience in CYW and consider a strengths-based model which strives to build community resilience.

We Hide Our Commitment to Critical Praxis

Ideas for critical praxis resonate with a conceptualisation of critical pedagogy which proposes education as the practice of freedom (Freire, 1970; 1996; hooks, 1994). In critical pedagogy, education is proposed as praxis which is understood as, 'action and reflection upon the world in order to change it' (Anglas Grande, 2009, p. 206).

Engaging in critical and problem-posing dialogue and reflection is coherent with Freirean pedagogy, whereby, the teacher is also a learner and the learner is also a teacher, in working together to create new knowledge. Framing education in the here and now, focussing on problems within real world situations as the means of raising consciousness and understanding, emphasises humanisation and the capacities of people to act in fellowship and solidarity with each other. Becoming conscious, not only of the world and the way knowledge is produced, but of our own capacities to produce new knowledge, and to change the world, is a core element of critical pedagogy (Giroux, 2005; Kincheloe, 2008; McLaren, 2009).

Throughout the United Kingdom, a commitment to critical praxis may be evident and underpins dialogical processes in CYW practice. Yet, this praxis is largely hidden from funders and people involved in policy development as practitioners seem to, somewhat understandably, aspire towards compliance rather than criticality, in order to sustain or secure funding or to demonstrate contribution to contemporary policy contexts. We will return to this topic in Chapter 9, in proposing border pedagogy as a threshold concept for sustaining CYW practice.

Next Steps: Making the 'Hidden Knowns' Visible

In seeking to understand the world, we need to see the historical constructions of power and the dominant culture in relationship to the everyday cultural experiences of people who are subordinate to those in power (McLaren, 2009). In regard to CYW practice we require these hidden knowns to be made visible and subject to discussion and critique. For example, in identifying three loosely coupled youth work practices, Coburn and Wallace (2011) proposed that one aspect, critical youth work, happens where:

> ... people are seen as capable social actors and citizens ... historical constructs and dominant ideologies are made visible ... people are encouraged to learn by probing common sense views of the world, to facilitate understanding of justice and injustice, power and oppression and ultimately, to promote social transformation ... work is political and participation in society is connected to democratic citizenship.
>
> Coburn and Wallace (2011, p. 15)

This is consistent with Ord (2016) in asserting that, 'youth work is necessarily critical and aspires towards social as well as individual change and transformation' (p. 228) and also with McIntyre (2014) who found that participation in critical Community Based Adult Learning (CBAL) engaged learners in processes that contributed to their health and well-being through supporting self-efficacy and feelings of agency. In this sense both youth work and CBAL, practiced as critical pedagogy, offer a counterbalance to dominant neo-liberal policy contexts that prioritise economic outcomes or impacts participation.

In the United States, these ideas have tended to inform debates around school education, and in seeking to address concerns about young people for whom schooling is a problem, or among communities that are impacted by poverty, discrimination and injustice. This view is consistent with the emancipatory curriculum proposed by Buchroth (2010) in the context of youth and community work in the United Kingdom where:

> Knowledge that is generated through an emancipatory curriculum is not a "commodity", it is not decided on beforehand and separated from the learner; instead it arises out of the process of learning itself ... what is learned arises from the process of questioning ... and learning is negotiated in a dialogical form between the learner and the teacher ... [as] ... co-investigators in the learning process.
>
> Buchroth (2010, p. 79)

Considering what we mean by 'hidden knowns', we propose that these could be used as a starting point for understanding how CYW can reclaim and reassert an emancipatory curriculum. There may be additional 'hidden knowns' that have been missed or are in need of further exploration.

In making these five 'hidden knowns' visible, we seek to strengthen development of a community of practice (Lave and Wenger, 1991; Wenger and Traynor, 2015) which in the area of CYW strives for a more equitable society. To establish CYW as a CoP the creation and development of artefacts, models and curricula by those currently involved in CYW is required. This is not only about supporting one particular professional field but rather a methodology that is part of an extended educational discipline. It is about reaching beyond current thinking to extend and develop new ideas for educational transformation among communities and for the transformation of education inside and beyond schooling.

Increasing transparency in regard to what we do, why we do it and how we do it, provides a basis in articulating our core purpose to those who are already involved in practice as participants or facilitators, and also to those who might seek to engage in practice in future. Generating a common discourse and making visible these 'hidden knowns', can unify and extend possibilities for thinking beyond current professional boundaries, to invigorate regional, national and international praxis.

Conclusion

Discussing the 'hidden knowns' as principles or values that underpin our professional identity, is particularly cogent in times where diversification of practice has created uncertainty and where funding and sustainability of previously routine practice contexts is impacted by current austerity measures. It is therefore important that we reassert our identity as purposeful and deliberate in striving for social change. Our next chapter considers core concepts of social justice and equality in order to contextualise our assertions about an emancipatory purpose for CYW, and how this might be realised in practice.

Bibliography

Anglas-Grande, S. M. (2009). American Indian geographies of identity and power: At the crossroads of Indigena and Mestizaje. In A. Darder, M. Baltodano and R. Torres (Eds.), *The Critical Pedagogy Reader* (pp. 183–208). Oxon: Routledge.

Baker, J., Lynch, K., Cantillion, S. and Walsh, J. (2004). *Equality: From Theory to Action.* Basingstoke: Palgrave Macmillan.

Batsleer, J. (2008). *Informal Learning in Youth Work.* London: Sage.

Buchroth, I. (2010) *Education*. In I. Buchroth and C. Parkin (Eds.), *Using Theory in Youth and Community Work Practice*. Exeter: Learning Matters.

Coburn, A and Gormally, S. (2014). Creating nexus for progressive pedagogy. *British Educational Research Association Conference*, Newman University, Birmingham, Presentation on 26 June 2014.

Coburn, A and Gormally, S. (2015). Emancipatory praxis: A social-justice approach to equality work. In C. Cooper, S. Gormally and G. Hughes (Eds.), *Socially-Just, Radical Alternatives for Education and Youth Work Practice: Re-Imagining Ways of Working with Young People*. Basingstoke: Palgrave MacMillan.

Coburn, A. (2012). Learning about equality: A study of a generic youth work setting. PhD thesis, University of Strathclyde. Accessed on 30 September 2016 at http://suprimo.lib. strath.ac.uk/primo_library/libweb/action/search.do

Coburn, A. and Wallace, D. (2011). *Youth Work in Communities and Schools*. Edinburgh: Dunedin Press.

Cooper, C., Gormally, S. and Hughes, G. (Eds.) (2015). *Socially-Just, Radical Alternatives for Education and Youth Work Practice: Re-Imagining Ways of Working with Young People*. Basingstoke: Palgrave MacMillan.

Davies, B. (2005). Youth work: A manifesto for our times. *Journal of Youth and Policy*, 88, 1–23.

Davies, B. (2015). Youth work: A manifesto for our times—Revisited. *Journal of Youth and Policy*, 114, 96–117.

Timpson, E. (2016). Department for education, funding boost for schools helping pupils develop character: Press Release. Accessed on 15 June 2016 at https://www.gov.uk/government/news/funding-boost-for-schools-helping-pupils-develop-character.

Freire, P. (1996). *Pedagogy of the Oppressed* (Ramos, M. B., Trans.) (2nd Ed.). London: Penguin.

Giroux, H. (2009). *Youth in a Suspect Society*. Basingstoke: Palgrave MacMillan.

Giroux, H. (2014). No bailouts for youth: Broken promises and dashed hopes. In S. Steinberg and A. Ibrahim (Eds.), *Critical Youth Studies Reader*. New York: Peter Lang.

Giroux, H. (2016). The mad violence of casino capitalism. *Counterpunch*. Retrieved at http://www.counterpunch.org/2016/02/19/the-mad-violence-of-casino-capitalism/

Glesne, C. (1989). Rapport and friendship in ethnographic research. *International Journal of Qualitative Studies in Education*, 2(1), 45–54.

Gallagher, S. and Morgan, A. (2013). The process is the product: Part one: Is there a need for measurement in youth work? *A Journal of Youth Work, Youthlink Scotland*, (11), 41–64. Accessed on 30 September 2016 at http://www.youthlinkscotland.org/Index.asp?MainID=9499

Ginwright, S. and Cammarota, J. (2002). New terrain in youth development: The promise of a social justice approach. *Social Justice*, 29(4), 84–95.

Gormally, S. and Coburn, A. (2014). Finding nexus: Connecting youth work and research practices. *British Educational Research Journal*, 40(50), 869–885.

hooks, b (1994). *Teaching to Transgress*. London: Routledge.

Jeffs, T. and Smith, M. K. (2005). *Informal Education, Conversation, Democracy and Learning* (3rd Ed.). Derby: Education Now.

Jeffs, T. and Smith, M. K. (Eds.) (2010) *Youth Work Practice*. Basingstoke: Palgrave Macmillan.

Kilmurray, A. (2017). *Community Action in a Contested Society: The Case of Northern Ireland.* Oxford: Peter Lang.

Kincheloe, J. (2008). *Critical Pedagogy* (2nd Ed.). New York: Peter Lang.

Lave, J. and Wenger, E. (1991). *Situated Learning: Legitimate Peripheral Participation.* Cambridge: Cambridge University Press.

Ledwith, M. (2016). *Community Development in Action: Putting Freire into Practice.* Bristol: Policy Press.

Ledwith, M. (2007). Reclaiming the radical agenda: A critical approach to community development. *Concept, 17*(2), 8–12.

Ledwith, M. (2011). *Community Development: A Critical Approach.* Bristol: The Policy Press.

McLaren, P. (2009). Critical pedagogy: A look at the major concepts. In A. Darder, M. Baltodano and R. Torres (Eds.), *The Critical Pedagogy Reader*, (pp. 183–208). Oxon: Routledge.

Martin, I. (2007). Reclaiming social purpose: Framing the discussion. *The Edinburgh Papers.* Edinburgh: Edinburgh University.

McIntyre, J. (2014). 'Right I can do this now': Community based adult learning, health and well-being. *Concept: The Journal of Contemporary Community Education Practice and Theory, 5*(3), pp. 12–20.

Ord, J. (2016). *Youth Work Process, Product and Practice: Creating an Authentic Curriculum in Work with Young People* (2nd Ed.). Oxon: Routledge.

Robertson, S (2005). *Youth Clubs: Association, Participation, Friendship and Fun*, Lyme Regis: Russell House Publishing.

Sen, A. (1985). Well-being, agency and freedom: The Dewey lectures 1984. *Journal of Philosophy, 82*, 169–221. Retrieved 10 May 2016 from http://www.freelogy.org/w/images/d/dc/Sen85.pdf

Sercombe, H. (2010). *Youth Work Ethics.* London: Sage.

Shaw, M. and McCulloch, K. (2009). Hooligans or rebels? Thinking more critically about citizenship and young people. *Journal of Youth and Policy*, No. 101, pp. 5–14.

Smith, M. K. (2002). Youth work: An introduction. *The Encyclopaedia of Informal Education*, www.infed.org/youthwork/b-yw.htm, accessed 24 May 2007.

Spence, J., Devanney, C., & Noonan, K. (2006). *Youth Work: Voices of Practice.* Leicester: National Youth Agency.

Taylor, T. (2008). Young people, politics and participation: A youth work perspective. *Journal of Youth and Policy*, 100, 253–263.

Taylor, T. (2010). Defending democratic youth work. *Concept, 1*(2), 3–10.

Tett, L. (2010). *Community Learning and Development* (3rd Ed.). Edinburgh: Dunedin Academic Press.

Wenger, E. (1998). *Communities of Practice: Learning, Meaning and Identity.* Cambridge: Cambridge University Press.

Wenger, E. and Traynor, B. (2015). Communities of practice: A brief introduction. Available at: http://wenger-trayner.com/wp-content/uploads/2015/04/07-Brief-introduction-to-communities-of-practice.pdf

Young, K. (2006). *The Art of Youth Work* (2nd Ed.). Lyme Regis: Russell House Publishing.

· 3 ·

SOCIAL JUSTICE AND EQUALITY

Introduction

This chapter explores concepts of social justice and equality that are vitally important when working with young people and adults within community development practice. Drawing on a value base of equality and social justice in youth work and community development practices (Davies, 2005; Jeffs and Smith, 2010; Smith, 2002; Taylor, 2010; Young, 2006), we assert a social and democratic purpose for emancipatory practice and consider conceptual distinctions and commonalities that help us to make a case for methodological praxis.

As CYW practitioners, we have encountered theoretical differences that challenged our purpose, our values and our methodological approaches. However, such differences were beneficial in prompting conversations that helped to confirm and challenge our personal, societal and world views and perspectives. Therefore we advocate that power sharing, negotiated dialogue, problem posing approaches and critical reflexivity can help practitioners to understand their own, and others, perspectives, in order to challenge and articulate practice. Defending our professional beliefs and rearticulating what our work is for, can assist CYW practitioners to reveal common goals which underpin the need for social change at micro and macro levels.

The chapter also analyses commonalities and contradictions that are important in contemporary political, structural and economic contexts (Giroux, 2014). In doing so, we seek to add a layer of discussion to the work of Cooper, Gormally, Hughes (2015), by unpicking aspects of emancipatory praxis in more detail in order to inform new possibilities for CYW practices.

Setting the Scene in Human Rights

Conceptualisations and discourses on equality have been developed over generations of theoretical and political debate. Yet, Thompson (2003) suggests that theorising how these ideas might be applied in social practices to promote equality, social justice and human rights is in the very early stages of development.

The United Nations Declaration of Human Rights states that, 'all people are born free and equal in dignity and rights' (United Nations, 1948). This promotes a discourse on equality that is based on a set of rights including human, social, cultural, economic and civil rights (Englund, Quennerstedt and Wahlstom, 2009). Thompson (2003) suggests that a human rights approach offers a way of addressing issues of inequality that may be useful to practitioners who are working with people to deal with their problems. Yet, while the rights and obligations of citizenship have been developed in schools and in youth work, Deuchar and Maitles (2007) have suggested that education for citizenship offers a limited hope for democracy in schools, and does not bring success for example, in the development of school pupil councils.

In Australia, Bessant (2007) found that calls for increased participation in decision making in youth work were countered by overt disapproval of young people's rights to engage in political protest. In the United Kingdom, there are paradoxes between a form of youth work that seeks to either control young people's behaviour or socialise them into society and one that seeks to engage them in active citizenship that liberates them from barriers to participation in order to promote possibilities for change (Coburn, 2011).

These paradoxes create tensions that are exemplified by Podd (2010) who, in examining local authority mechanisms for youth participation, found that although young people's participation was extended across many areas of public policy, the capacity for this to enhance democracy and youth empowerment was limited within the present social systems and structures. The use of traditional methods, such as youth councils or consultation events was suggested as problematic, especially when these consultations were based on pre-set agendas, in areas defined as Children's Service Plans or antisocial behaviour (Podd, 2010, p. 25). Podd concludes that there is a lack of shared understanding about what is meant by participation and empowerment. In particular, she suggests that the roots of participation in democracy and social justice, and of empowerment as the means through which young people can challenge social structures, have become lost:

> The radical objectives of 'participation' may have been replaced by a participatory policy rooted in maintaining social control over the disenfranchised, who are historically and persistently viewed as either problematic or in need ... [and for young people] ... the barriers and challenges thus remain largely unchanged from those of a decade ago.
>
> Podd (2010, p. 31)

Thus, while human rights work contributes to the development of a fairer and more equal society, it appears that these rights do not go far enough in seeking the level of social change needed for young people to participate equally and to be respected as equal citizens. Shaw and McCulloch have also argued:

> If young people are seen or constructed in particular ways, then those ways of seeing them might have quite different consequences for the way in which citizenship is seen in relation to *them*—and to what being a citizen might mean.
>
> Shaw and McCulloch (2009, p. 7)

Shaw and McCulloch (2009) further suggest current understandings of empowerment as 'simplistic propaganda' (p. 7) put forward by successive Governments and have suggested a need to 'think more critically about the relationship between citizenship, democracy and the political lives of young people' (p. 8). They propose the creation of a political culture as the route through which to challenge inequality and that 'in the face of injustice, exploitation or inequality, it could be argued that dissenting is the only responsible thing to do' (p. 11), in order to assist those who are furthest away from power to imagine how they might participate in democracy.

This adds to what Bessant (2007) has highlighted in discussion of the UN Convention. She reminds us that Article 12 requires children under the age of 18 'to have the right to say what they think should happen, when adults are making decisions that affect them, and to have their opinions taken into account' (United Nations, 1989). Yet, she suggests that while the UN

Convention has clarified the rights of children and young people to play a full part in society, these rights are open to interpretation in the practices and institutions that take forward services for young people.

Similarly, Englund et al. (2009) have highlighted a tension between parental rights on the education of their children, and the UN Convention on the Rights of the Child (United Nations, 1989), that seeks to strengthen young people's rights in relation to their own education. Rights conferred on adults could, in some instances, contradict the rights of young people, under the UN Convention. They suggest that this raises questions of whose view would be privileged in any dispute and open debate on the relationship between different sets of rights.

In this sense, a rights discourse may be useful as a means of ensuring basic entitlements and as a starting point in the journey towards equality. Yet, there remains a question of which view would be taken in situations where there were competing or conflicting interests. Nor does the question of equality reconcile with a human rights discourse for young people if they are also subject to the effects of a powerful discourse that means they may not always be able to assert those rights. For example, full citizenship rights are routinely withheld until young people reach the age of 21 (Fulcher and Scott, 2007). In light of this position, our focus turns to Social Justice and Equality as a means of generating social change.

Social Justice

Rawls (1971) proposed that a series of social contracts clarifies how social relations are developed and enable society to function. This includes, for example, political contracts between governments and citizens or economic contracts between employers and employees. Rawls proposed that the success of these contracts and the social structure of society were reliant on a liberal ideology that argued for a fairer society, 'on the grounds that the desire to avoid poverty is greater than the attraction of riches' (Heywood, 2007, p. 57). Rawls (1971) claimed that this would bring social justice by creating a fairer world and proposed two principles for fairness.

Fernandez (2000) examined Rawls' two principles for justice as fairness. The first principle was related to liberty and meant that people should be able to exercise their personal rights to free thinking and to exercising moral powers. The second principle was about equality of opportunity, meaning that people of similar ability or social class, would have a fair chance of making the same life as anyone else.

These principles of justice are rooted in individuals rather than in communities or governments. Fernandez (2000) notes the introduction of what Rawls called the 'difference principle' which proposed that the benefits of social justice should be accrued by the most disadvantaged. This brings implications in terms of the development of public policy, for example in targeting the use of public resources to ensure the welfare of people living in the most disadvantaged communities.

Despite the drive towards a positive view of young people as evidenced in the European Impetus for Youth (European Commission, 2001), there is little evidence of any new social or political developments that create and invest in a positive view of young people, on which to legislate for change. This suggests that significant structural changes are needed if young people are to take control over important aspects of their lives.

These ideas have shown the contested nature of social justice which is set within a context that is neither fixed nor static (Capeheart and Milovanovic, 2007). Centrally it is about identifying and attempting to address structural disadvantage, discrimination and inequality by refocusing on process, participation and collective rights. As noted previously (Coburn and Gormally, 2015), social justice can be seen as redistribution of resources and goods and the politics of recognition (Fraser, 2009, Lister, 2008). Burchardt and Craig (2008, p. 12) assert:

> Theories of social justice help to identify and classify different aspects of a person's life with which we should be concerned: the extent to which their basic needs are met, the resources available to them relative to others, their negative and positive freedoms, their status, and the degree of recognition they receive, to name but a few.

Nevertheless, the term has been used in a range of contexts and is aligned with a number of philosophical traditions. The working group on Philanthropy for Social Justice and Peace invited funders from around the world to provide their own explanation of social justice work. Ruesga and Puntenney (2010) concluded there were eight central traditions:

1. Structural injustice
2. Universal human rights
3. Fairness/equality distribution of resources

4. Legalism/rule of law
5. Empowerment
6. Shared values
7. Cultural relativism
8. Triple bottom line

These eight central traditions provide a framework for discussion.

1. Structural Injustice

As educational youth workers and community development practitioners, an awareness of the social structures and processes that exist in cultural, educational, financial and legal institutions is essential to understanding the breadth of influences that combine to sustain structural inequality and injustice. Ledwith and Springett (2010, p. 27) note:

> The structural level [is] where social divisions are sewn into the fabric of society and oppression and discrimination become institutionalised.

Engaging in critical reflection of structural disadvantage enables practitioners to raise critical consciousness about how this impacts on communities who experience poverty and deprivation. Dominant ideology is embedded in structures, which in turn impact on the cultural and personal aspects of life (Thompson, 1997). The normalisation of structural injustice can then result in a lack of criticality about the impact:

> Since the dominant ideology is embedded in our institutional practices and individual consciousness, for oppression to continue we just need to act "normally", to go along with the status quo.
>
> Goodman (2011, p. 18)

This idea of going along with the status quo means that unless community and youth workers are critically conscious to the structural injustices apparent within societies the default position is to do nothing. Operating individually reduces the chances for social change because people are inclined to maintain the status quo. This is clearly problematic in areas such as human rights, where for example, people may not know that they have rights or have the capability to assert their rights, and where maintaining the status quo could be seen as collusion with those whose interests are served by injustice.

2. Universal Human Rights

The Declaration of Human Rights (1948) provides a set of fundamental rights that have to be protected for all peoples and nations. Although there is commonality between human rights and social justice, there are clear differences. As Meckled-Garcia (2011, p. 29) asserts:

> Running together human rights and social justice standards not only blurs their distinctive features, it diminishes their distinctive contributions to our moral repertoire.

While human rights are a foundational basis for individual rights, which are undoubtedly important, social justice adopts a collective approach. It is important to understand the distinction between human rights, as an individually focussed foundational entitlement that creates possibilities for making a good life (Sen, 1985), while social justice takes a collective focus on inequality and how it might be eradicated:

> The conception of social justice … [when] … used within this community development context seeks to address and focus upon the collective broader rights for groups and communities whilst still recognising that the rights of the individual should not be negated nor ignored by the collective.
>
> Gormally (2012, p. 18)

Yet, recognition of these entitlements does not in itself bring equality and this raises questions about distribution.

3. Fairness/Equality Distribution of Resources

If the redistribution of resources and goods is concerned with challenging the societal norm whereby some people have a lot of resources while others have considerably less, it is clear that any attempt at creating a fairer distribution will be resisted by those who stand to lose the most. Dorling (2013) explains that since 2008 there is an increasingly growing gap between the wealthiest 1% and the rest in the United Kingdom. However, social justice does not solely focus on 'equality of status' but on the 'equality of outcome'. Providing people with a fair opportunity is not sufficient in ensuring a socially just society:

> Technically, all full citizens have equality of status within a society; however, equality of opportunity and access, and of outcome—say, for black minority ethnic groups, or for women—are clearly not present in any society.
>
> Craig (2005, p. 3)

If a structure is inherently unjust and unequal, then having opportunity within that structure will not produce a just society. For example, equality of opportunity, suggests that people should be able to have an equal chance of achieving social position through merit. This appears as a popular conception of equality in literature (Merton et al., 2004) and in youth work policy (Scottish Executive, 2007). Yet, equality of opportunity has been criticised as a 'survival of the fittest mentality ... dismissed as a "tadpole philosophy", highlighting the struggle for survival amongst tadpoles as they develop into frogs' (Heywood, 2007, p. 106). Thus, unless people's starting points are equal at the outset, simply having access to a range of opportunities does not in itself, make a difference to people who experience inequality.

Thus, the notion of a just society is highly debated and political. It can be linked to 'human rights, human dignity and the common good' (Ruesga and Puntenney, 2010, p. 10) but this can change depending on the government in control, the laws and the normalised perceptions of what is 'good' for the citizens. For the purposes of this book, it is worth highlighting that despite the contested nature of this approach we also argue that practitioners should strive for more equal outcomes by advocating a redistribution of resources and goods. This will require changes to the present systems and structures that support social justice and will include the movement of resources from those with most to those with least. As Ruesga and Puntenney (2010, p. 10) note:

> ... redistribution will likely cause resentment for some, while adjusting systems to distribute resources more equally from the outset will be slightly less controversial, if only because the manipulations will be less visible.

Despite this, the underpinning purpose of our work should still be to work towards a more socially just society and to imagine new possibilities, irrespective of the controversy it may cause. Analysing how this is done and how policy is targeted to support those most marginalised (Lister, 2008; Young, 2008) is also a key part of being an effective practitioner.

4. Legalism/Rule of Law

Following Rawls (1971) principles for social justice, the 'legalism and rule of law' approach suggests that 'social justice consists of protecting marginalized communities through the rigorous enforcement of existing laws' (Ruesga and Puntenney, 2010, p. 11). Although laws should be equally applied and utilised, this does not mean that all laws are equitable or just. Yet, critics of Rawls' (1971) theory have centred on the discordant nature of using compulsory legislative structures to create fairness and freedom and in emphasising the individual rather than community or social group (Tower Sargent, 2006). Indeed, Deuchar (2009) has argued that legislation may discriminate against young people in the development of regulatory policies and in the passing of laws that criminalise routine activity such as hanging around the streets.

Baker et al. (2004) have also critiqued Rawls' argument for fair and equal opportunity, regardless of social class, as it appears to both accept and challenge the existence of a class division, and in particular have noted that Rawls' theory of social justice 'is also notorious for its neglect of gender' (Baker et al. 2004, p. 42).

This stance suggests that laws should be value free. However, the application of these are not always so. Although a legal understanding of equality and justice is important, this book does not focus on this view of social justice in detail. Instead our focus is to analyse how youth work and community development practice can be utilised to bring about social change, not to assess the legal frameworks in which it operates. (For further details about youth work law see McGinley, 2014).

5. Empowerment

The tradition of empowerment and analysis of power relations are core concepts in community practices. Working alongside communities and young people, as part of those communities, in order to facilitate individual and community advocacy and to create conditions for a fair and just society is crucial to community development practices. Set within a tradition of empowerment, social justice advocates for people to have recognition of voice and also the capacity, power and ability, to utilise that voice when necessary (Lister, 2008). Chapter 5 offers a detailed examination of power and empowerment to show why, it is necessary for practitioners to have a clear understanding of power in order to facilitate empowerment. This tradition is important because empowerment is not something that can be granted with a magic wand, instead it is a process of analysing power relations and assessing the way in which these can be challenged, encouraged or negotiated.

6. Shared Values

This tradition is grounded in the belief that shared values can foster cohesion and motivation. Although the creation of shared values may not be straight-forward, these may be something to strive for. If those in privileged groups can comprehend the benefits of a more equitable and just society then oppression and discrimination can be eliminated. Goodman asserts, 'I would like people from privileged groups to be committed to being allies and able to act in soli-darity with people from oppressed groups (and others from privileged groups) to promote equity' (Goodman, 2011 p. 5). This may seem naïve or utopian, but that shift toward a more equitable future may rely on attempts to gain a sense of shared values.

7. Cultural Relativism

Recognition of cultural difference is vital in community work. Understand-ing peoples' starting points and experiences of diverse and complex cultural contexts underpins their capabilities for creating social change. Theoretically, seeing culture in relation to a given context can be helpful in understand-ing or interpreting why things are the way they are. This means that unless we understand the cultural values and beliefs of the communities we work with, and can see things from perspectives that are different to our own, we cannot begin to work with people in ways that are socially just. Yet, cultural relativism is critiqued, particularly by feminist scholars, for accepting or ratio-nalising practices and social values that may be inherently discriminating or unjust, if simply based on cultural reasoning and essentialist views on cultures (Narayan, 2000; Nussbaum, 1999).

Nussbaum's perspective on capability 'encourages us to encounter and learn from other cultures and societies in an effort to move towards a shared account of the core human capabilities' (Clark, 2006, p. 7). Nussbaum (2003) suggests that everyone should have the freedom and capability to participate in a good life. Thus, cultural practices that repress voice and freedom and promote discrimination, oppression or injustice among particular groups in society should not be accepted simply because they are part of a particular or dominant culture. Awareness of the cultural environment is therefore impera-tive to the creation of a culturally appropriate pedagogy that may also be used to change oppressive conditions through challenging or accepting cultural practices and difference. Cultural relativism offers a frame for conversations about social justice in areas that can be particularly complex and fragile, needing careful and skilled negotiation with community members.

8. Triple Bottom Line

This tradition is premised on the argument that businesses could be socially responsible and could facilitate well-being with a focus on 'people, planet and profit'. It is where corporate interests can overlap and intersect with societal ones (Savitz, 2013) to mean that the market can have a role in reducing injustice whilst promoting sustainability and development. Starting from a basis of people and planet as well as profit can be useful in shifting towards increased cooperation and to creation of shared values on why social justice is important. However, a neo-liberal policy agenda married with capitalism makes us sceptical on the capacity to strive for true social justice which redistributes resources as a means of achieving a more equitable society. (For more detailed discussion on triple bottom line, see Henriques and Richardson, 2004).

This eight-point framework highlights some of the key philosophical traditions that inform understanding of the concept of social justice. Achieving social change requires understanding of those philosophical traditions in order to strive for a society that promotes both justice of recognition and justice of economic distribution (Atkinson, 2015; Fraser, 2009; Lister, 2008). This raises critical questions for CYW practice about how to engage with groups in working towards a conceptualisation of social justice that requires us to recognise inequalities and to redistribute power in order to achieve a fairer world. An additional layer of complexity, is found in questions about how the concept of equality underpins the establishment of emancipatory praxis in community work, that help communities to explore the prerequisites for fair recognition, as Craig notes, 'Social justice has a strong relationship with – but is not the same thing as – equality' (2008, p. 2).

Scullion (2011) has created a helpful table to differentiate between the two concepts of Social Justice and Human Rights.

Created for a community development project in Northern Ireland (Gormally, 2012), this table demonstrates a practical framework for implementation of social justice. It also contextualises the need for both redistribution of resources and goods as well as the politics of recognition. Redistribution of resources is premised in a stance that identifies particular types of society, namely capitalist societies, as inherently unjust. Redistribution would ensure equality of economy across nation states globally. In Fig 2 the redistribution

Human Rights	Social Justice
Focus is on the rights of the individual	Focus is on the community and collective action; focus is on process
In NI, human rights have underpinned the mechanisms of legal court cases supported by institutions (PILS/ NIHRC/ECNI, etc.) to challenge decision-making	Emphasis is on **process** of building participation and challenging injustice both at state and community level
Strongest rights are civic and political rights; weakest rights are economic, social and cultural rights	Mainly concerned with social and economic inequalities
Challenges **state power**—state is the duty bearer	Challenges **all sources of power**—private sector, state and individuals in communities
Orientated towards making state bodies act in accordance with their human rights obligations	Yes, but **broader approach** as human rights obligations do not apply to private bodies, e.g., communities and individuals, funders, private sector bodies, churches etc.
Orientated towards court challenges, i.e., judicial review of state actions/ decisions	Process involves a broader range of challenges to, for example: • Internal injustices, e.g., exclusion of certain groups within 'the community'—women, young, old, disabled, BME, gay, non-Irish nationals, different political viewpoints etc. • Exclusion of the voices of such groups in decision-making • Challenges community/collective decision making processes • External injustices include negative perception of the community by others (statutory agencies, politicians, media, other communities) and injustice in inequitable allocation of resources—jobs, health, housing
Positive human rights outcomes include: • Changes in law or government policies, e.g., following Art 8 complaint re lack of effective access to abortion facilities in Republic of Ireland, ECtHR ordered law to be changed for benefit of all women • Access to rights for individuals and therefore for others, e.g., right of domestic violence survivors to be protected by the state following Arts 2 and 3 complaint	Laws may change (as result of HR legal challenges), but doesn't always translate into action that improves the lives of disadvantaged people. Social justice creates: • Opportunity to make groups more accountable, tackle gate-keeping, tackle real and perceived injustices • Framework for understanding systems, power and power relationships • New opportunities for community development created by inclusion of wider range of voices • New opportunities to build solidarity within and with other communities

Figure 2. Some Differences between Social Justice and Human Rights. Scullion (2011, p. 23).

of resources is evident in the focus on social and economic inequalities as opposed to solely civic and political rights. Importantly at a local level, there needs to be an analysis of the " ... inequitable allocation of resources – jobs, health, housing etc" (Scullion, 2011, p. 23).

The importance of a politics of recognition is evident both at micro and macro levels. On a micro level, this is apparent when analysing internal injustices with the exclusion of particular groups, the exclusion of voices within these groups and the restrictions placed on particular groups in decision making. This exclusion can be evident internally within a community or externally from one community to another. On a macro level, recognition is shown in the representation and negative perceptions of particular communities by those in positions of power, including politicians, media and statutory agencies.

Having examined conceptualisations of Human Rights, we now consider how this relates to conceptualisations of equality.

Equality

Whilst social justice focuses upon equality of opportunity and the outcome of that opportunity; equality has also been identified as the ability to deal with situations and to have the agency to take decisions forward (Baker et al. 2004). People's capacity to deal with their own situations is influenced by how they are positioned in relationship to the rest of society and to each other. Atkinson notes:

> The reduction of inequality should be a priority for everyone ... Inequality is embedded in our social and economic structure, and a significant reduction requires us to examine all aspects of our society.
>
> Atkinson (2015, p. 3)

In the United Kingdom, young people are routinely found to be 'at the bottom of the scale of power ... [and] ... have norms, rules and definitions of order imposed upon them' (Hamilton and Seymour, 2006, p. 63). While, among an increasingly older population Taylor (2010) has argued for increased involvement of communities in social welfare. This lack of participation in decisions about their lives, makes it difficult for people to take forward their own aims and actions. In studying equality, Baker et al (2004) suggest that a focus on particular social groups who experience inequalities offers scope for collective action for social change.

Sen (1985; 1999) theorised equality as capability, building on a conceptualisation that well-being depends on the capabilities of people to achieve agency in their capacities to do things, and to achieve their own goals. Importantly, capability is about people's capacity to function well, and should not be restricted to a limited set of functions that are within their reach. Sen argued that if one person has the same capability to function as another, then they each have the 'freedom to live well … [and] … the freedom to achieve well-being' (Sen, 1985, p. 200). This facilitates involvement at a micro, individual level but for a more socially just society inclusion in challenging structural inequalities is also important.

Baker et al. (2004) argue that liberal egalitarianism falls short of the mark because it does not challenge inequalities that persist and so, more needs to be done to rebuild and reconfigure dominant social structures, which can be aligned with challenging structural injustice. Equality of condition takes basic equality, expressed in terms of human and social rights to food and shelter, as the starting point for discussion. Yet, as noted earlier, these basic entitlements are not a satisfactory way of ensuring fair distribution of resources because they emphasise redistribution without recognition (Lister, 2008) resulting in access to resources that fulfil basic needs but does not bring a more socially just society.

A liberal egalitarian perspective, such as the historical position taken in literature on social justice (Rawls, 1971) is argued by Baker et al. (2004) as helping to manage inequality rather than contributing to its eradication. For example, in being concerned with how equally resources are competed for, rather than how they can be fairly distributed.

Taking an alternative social egalitarian perspective, underpinned by cooperation and solidarity, equality of condition aims to 'eliminate major inequalities altogether or at least massively to reduce the current scale of inequality' (Baker et al., 2004, p. 33). This can be achieved by distinguishing between fairness in the competition for advantage (liberal egalitarianism) and fairness in the freedom of choice that people have in life (social egalitarianism).

This distinction is grounded in the argument that fairness of opportunity, through competing with others, does not bring fairness of choice, and indeed may limit the choices of those who are unable to compete, or who do not win the competition. Equality of condition addresses these concerns by seeking to change the rules in society, so that everyone has a fair and free choice to live their lives in the way they want. In theorising equality of condition, Baker et al. (2004) offer five dimensions of equality:

1. Respect and recognition
2. Resources
3. Love, care and solidarity
4. Power
5. Working and learning as equals

Each of these dimensions offers insights about the extent to which equality may be identified as present in a particular setting or situation and can be used to consider the extent to which youth and community work enhances people's sense of well-being in order to create a liberating praxis.

Respect and recognition—Respect and recognition in this sense aligns closely with politics of recognition (Lister, 2008). This is not about tolerating difference but celebrating it (Baker et al., 2004). They advocate for criticality in examination of dominant culture whilst also facilitating the capacity of those who dominate to listen to subordinate groups. In advocating for social equality the need for recognition in governance and status of citizens in democratic processes is also asserted, for example, in having the capacity to voice opinion and the right to say something about making a life (Lister, 2008). Moreover, the capacity to hold people accountable when necessary is a key strand in a democratically equal society. For those experiencing unjust inequality there is a need to take additional steps (Young, 2008) to achieve both respect and recognition through the process of empowerment.

Resources—The need for resources and goods in a general sense should be more equally accepted overall. This perspective advocates for a change in the distribution of wealth and income and that access to public services is reviewed in order to promote equality. However, not all those fighting for equality would go as far as social justice in the attempt to redress the economic inequalities and rather:

> ... liberal egalitarians take inequality of resource to be inevitable, they are concerned to ensure that competition for advantage is as fair as possible and that it is governed by equal opportunity.
>
> Baker et al. (2004, p. 27)

Practically, inequality of resources may seem inevitable but theoretically, there can be a considerable movement towards redressing such inevitabilities. Current conditions should not prevent us from striving towards a better future. Moreover, in countries where there are vast income inequalities social stratification becomes more important (Wilkinson and Pickett, 2010). As Young (2008, p. 79) asserts:

> Persons suffer injustice by virtue of structural inequality when their group social positioning means that the operation of diverse institutions and practices conspires to limit their opportunities to achieve well-being.

Thus, it is important to analyse the social resources available given that this can directly link to one's sense of good health and subjective well-being.

Love, care and solidarity—This emphasises the wellbeing of self and others in our practice. The act of caring can be explained as '… an activity and an attitude' (Baker et al., 2004, p. 37). As practitioners, our capacity to 'care' is hugely important. This is not only caring for others but caring for oneself as a worker. Current policy reform, particularly within England, has actively eroded 'care' through welfare reforms (Hughes, Cooper, Gormally and Rippingale, 2014) and is in danger of promoting inequality and furthering social tensions and problems (Wilkinson and Pickett, 2009). Irrespective, community development and youth work practitioners continue to demonstrate care, love and solidarity. However, as Hughes et al. (2014) demonstrate there is a danger that there becomes a privileging of care for others over self-care. Placing this in the wider policy context, Abramovitz and Zelnick (2010, p. 113) suggest:

> The shared interests of care workers and the people they care for in the 'fight back' against neoliberalism suggest the potential for aligning care workers' health and safety with client/patient needs in public policy formation. The health and safety of care workers in the global economy is an important dimension for evaluating public policies and envisioning better ones.

As practitioners, we need to demonstrate care for ourselves, colleagues and those we work with. In addition, solidarity involves actively supporting each other and demonstrating cohesion in the struggles being faced. Although this analysis may be interpreted as a minor point in striving for a more equitable and just society it creates shared values and cohesion in this endeavour. Desmond Tutu (Tutu in Barasch, 2005) asserts that compassion and love are not passive acts but acts of action:

> Compassion is not just feeling with someone, but seeking to change the situation. Frequently people think compassion and love are merely sentimental. No! They are very demanding. If you are going to be compassionate, be prepared for action!
>
> Barasch (2005)

This highlights more than just monetary equality and rather demonstrates that improvement in our quality of life is as much about 'community and how we relate to each other' (Wilkinson and Pickett, 2010, p. 254) and so in striving for equality, the idea of love, care and solidarity is important.

Power—According to Tawney (1964, p. 158), 'Power is the most obvious characteristic of an organised society, but it is also the most ambiguous'. This view of equality was based on three key areas:

- A dispersion of power so that no one can wield power over another person and people can work co-operatively for the common social purpose;
- A social function that means property rights are dependent on obligations to promote happiness and social good, which offers a way of organising society for common good, as different from a capitalist society that is organised through goals that are achieved in the pursuit of gain;
- A democratic citizenship connects power and authority to public good and citizenship to a shared life and set of relationships that connect the personal and the political, in purpose and process ... commitment combined with a collective effort for the common good of humanity.

Adapted from Smith (2007)

Building on this early work, Baker et al., (2009) see analysis of power as a two-fold approach. They assert that firstly, dominant groups can hold unchallenged power resulting in oppression and secondly, that power can exist in other areas such as education, religion, family and the economy. Both of these levels must be challenged. Of particular relevance in educational youth and community work contexts, democratizing education sits at the heart of this challenge. Education is never politically neutral. As previously noted, corporate infiltration of schools is problematic in perpetuating a particular ideological stance. Yet, at a more fundamental level schools have been perpetuating inequalities of power in the stratification of students and privileging of particular kinds of knowledge, whereby students are positioned as powerful or powerless (Baker et al., 2009) The topic of power and empowerment is fundamental to our practice and as such will be discussed in detail in Chapter 5.

Working and learning as equals—Work in itself is not equal, with many types of responsibilities not recognised as work due to being personal, unpaid, and unsupported—for example, caring responsibilities. Essentially, Baker et al. (2009) suggest that 'the overall benefits and burdens of work should be as equal as possible' (p. 40). This does not mean that everyone does the same job but that everyone has a fair chance of benefiting from the work that they do.

Wilkinson and Pickett (2010, p. 237) also note:

> Greater equality is the gateway to a society capable of improving the quality of life for all of us and an essential step in the development of a sustainable economic system.

In working and learning as equals, the focus is on the creation of possibilities for each person to learn and be employed, in order to contribute to the economic system, in whatever way that system is configured. Thus, the idea of equality is not restricted to, nor limited by, existing capitalism, and indeed, Baker et al (2004) would argue that equality will only be possible when there is radical social change in how society is constructed.

Contradictions and Cohesion

Although there are clearly areas of commonality and cohesion in discussing equality and social justice and the possibilities for an alternative vision for the world, these are not the same. Rawls (1971) felt that justice incorporated equality in so far as his second and third principle of social justice noted the importance of equality of opportunity and equality of 'primary goods'. Having inequality of primary goods, including income, wealth and the social bases of respect was only allowed if it was to benefit the worst off in society (Burchardt and Craig, 2008, p. 4).

Social justice, in this simplistic analysis, focuses more on a collective, macro analysis whilst equality also discusses micro levels of engagement in order to achieve a more equitable society. Social Justice now focuses a dual politics of recognition and redistribution (Young, 1990). However, as Fraser (1997) notes the politics of recognition should not override the need for redistribution and class analysis. Fraser (1997) argued that recognition may seek to celebrate and acknowledge differences while redistribution was an attempt to prevent differences. Arguably, there is the capacity to do both. Fraser in later work (2009) moved from analysing group misrecognition as about identity to 'social status subordination and status' (Lister, 2002, p. 41), thus aiding an analysis of poverty. However, the celebration of difference can be beneficial in practice. It does not prevent justice and equality; rather it can facilitate cohesion and understanding, while promoting action.

Equality can be viewed as coming from two distinct traditions—equality of opportunity or equality of outcome. Equality of opportunity is concerned with creating a 'level playing field' while outcome is about what happens thereafter. Equality of opportunity is not sufficient for creation of a more socially just society. In reimagining a new social world, equality of outcome is necessary. Atkinson (2015) argues that whilst equality of opportunity may be alluring, creating an equal basis, there is a need to focus on both equality of opportunity and equality of outcome. 'Inequality of outcome among today's generation is the source of unfair advantage received by the next generation. If we are concerned about equality of opportunity tomorrow, we need to be concerned about inequality of outcome today' (Atkinson, 2015, p. 11). This aligns with the notion that social inequalities need to be challenged and a reassessment of the systems which reproduce inequalities would be helpful. Rawls (2001) argued that social justice was generally about reducing inequalities while equality of condition recognises that '... inequality is rooted in changing and changeable social structures and particularly in structures of domination and oppression' (Baker et al., 2004, p. 33). Being critical of structural domination and relating this to practice is important in CYW practices. It offers a reassessment of society as a whole and opens up the opportunity to imagine new ways of working that are more equal and just for all.

So, despite differences in focus across social justice and equality literature, we argue that these two concepts do assist in creating conditions for a better society; a society that is capable of equitable outcomes and that considers knowledge and understanding and the acceptance of difference as a foundation for social change. This leads to our central argument that community development and educational youth work requires that practitioners articulate the purpose of their work as contributing to a wider movement for social change. Our assertion is that theory on social justice and equality are aligned in showing that structural disadvantage, discrimination and inequality must be challenged and addressed (Coburn and Gormally, 2015). This is achieved through dual practices that analyse the redistribution of economic resources and also engages with communities in order to work with them to facilitate improved conditions.

Together, this mix of critical analysis and engagement builds community capability through acknowledging the importance of recognition in achieving liberating practice, which is multifaceted. This involves recognition of collective rights whilst including individual differences and perspectives. Such practice is underpinned by analysis of power relations in: respect and recognition; delivery and distribution of resources; health and wellbeing (love, care and solidarity) and working and learning (Baker et al., 2004). Liberating practice is achieved by promoting and recognising voice and identity, by revaluing the undervalued, devalued or ignored identities that are aligned with exclusion and prejudice, and an appreciation that lack of recognition as well as health and well-being are often intertwined and heightened in cases of material deprivation (Coburn and Gormally, 2015).

Theory into Practice

Throughout this chapter, we have analysed theoretical approaches to social justice and equality. Social justice and equality work have a slightly different focus but are still intrinsically linked, where 'social justice is the core value of youth work' (Crooks, 1992, p. 20) and youth workers commit to, 'the Freirian notion … of remedying social inequality' (Corney, 2004, p. 522). Yet:

> Rather than being a mechanistic enterprise, offering formulas and recipes, theory should provide the frameworks and tools for what it means to be a thoughtful, judicious, layered, complex and critical thinker willing to engage in communicative and collective action.
>
> Giroux (2014)

In order to engage in theoretically informed practice and a theorising of CYW practice as emancipatory praxis, practitioners need to have a critical understanding of both macro and micro levels of injustice and inequality to effectively work in redressing these. However, in practice terms, Sen (2009) argues that the best place to start with social justice is with people's lives and to concentrate on 'redressable injustices'. These are injustices that can be addressed and achieved. They are the relatively small-scale injustices that can still have an impact on the communities and groups in which we work. Starting from a point where people can see 'quick wins' builds confidence and trust. It ensures that action is seen as productive and not futile. If we do not begin with redressable injustices, which have been identified by engaging with people who live and work in the communities we work in, this can result in feelings of failure, a lack of trust in the process and in feeling like the mountain is just too big to climb.

An understanding of the macro levels of inequality is essential, but when working with community groups and young people, a good starting point often begins with 'redressable injustices' (Sen, 2009; Gormally, 2012) which help to build confidence and foster critical awareness. At a micro-level promoting 'small wins' helps to facilitate understanding of power imbalances and to find ways to critique and challenge these. The language of possibility and a belief in personal and collective power can gradually begin to move people forward on a continuum towards a more equal and just society. As Blackburn (2008, p. 256) notes:

> ... we would have huge difficulty in defining total equality, let alone recognising it. However, this is not a reason for abandoning concern about social inequality.

Working towards this goal can take differing forms. In community development, this work can include encouraging groups to reflect on their situations, analyse options and then act on their reflections. There is a need to raise consciousness of social and economic inequalities and to provide people with the capabilities, opportunities and resources to take action to address the inequalities they face (Gormally, 2012). It is also necessary for practitioners to understand theory and put this into practice, while in turn, learning from the practice to implement theory and in doing so create praxis (Freire, 1970). This liberating practice includes a challenge function. Challenge is purposeful in facilitating a critique of social inequalities, and questioning 'common sense' norms, to generate alternative views of societal/community possibilities. To help raise critical consciousness of inequalities a negotiated process is needed in working with communities. As professional practitioners, we seek to promote collective social rights—the right of communities to express their voice, to challenge poverty and social exclusion, to challenge what is being done 'to' or 'for' them as a community and to encourage a re-imagining of new possibilities for justice.

Practitioners have to become 'critical friends' (Gormally, 2012) and develop skills in what Thompson (2003) calls 'elegant challenging' (p. 226). This involves being constructive and creating conditions where it is OK for people to 'save face' while being challenged. It includes selecting an appropriate time and place for the challenge and being assertive not aggressive. It also acknowledges that while being genuine in seeking to promote social justice and equality, the 'challenger' may sometimes 'get it wrong' or be discriminating. So, elegant challenging requires a confident yet empathetic approach of both informed challenge and supportive understanding. Further, we would suggest that such challenging cannot take place prior to the building of rapport, questioning, being critically reflective and supportive. These skills are also useful in building relationships for equality. Fundamentally, it is necessary to listen to the voices of people and their experience of services (Rudnick et al, 2014) and policy to find ways of addressing apparent injustices. Yet, experiences of injustice and inequality are subjective and contextualised. As such, the voice of those experiencing injustice must be valued and their experiences of discrimination acted upon.

Conclusion

Building on examination of existing literature on social justice and equality (Baker et al., 2004; Craig et al, 2008; Rawls, 1971, 2001; Fraser, 1997, 2009; Sen, 1985; 2009), we agree with these authors in arguing that if we are serious committed to achieving a more equal and just society then we need social change. As Giroux (2014) notes:

> Such change will not come unless the call for political and economic change is matched by a change in subjectivity, consciousness and the desire for a better world.

It is our assertion that youth and community practitioners can contribute to exploration of aspects of social justice and equality when working with communities. Enabling communities and practitioners to grapple with these concepts and to consider how to put them into practice helps to tease out the complexities of praxis.

This chapter has demonstrated theoretical approaches to equality and social justice and draws comparison between the two. This offers a means for a range of professional and disciplinary areas to assess their own practice as the context for an emancipatory purpose. Framing practice in this way promotes and develops work that is embedded in a commitment to the struggle for equality and social justice.

This chapter has problematised concepts of social justice and equality in seeking to incorporate imagination and utopian thinking into practice. It allows us to problematise our current social structures and to think practically of ways to engage with communities to self-advocate for a more equal and just society. In thinking about why we work in the way we do, the promotion of critical reflection offers a continual challenge of ourselves and others. This promotes possibilities for working within, and outside, of current discourse to create new ideas or alternative forms of knowledge (Giroux, 2005). In suggesting liberating community praxis, we dare to dream, and to work towards, a more socially just and equal world. The next chapter examines the concept of community as the context through which such purposeful practice is developed.

Bibliography

Abramovitz, M. and Zelnick, J. (2010). Double jeopardy: The impact of neoliberalism on care workers in the United States and South Africa. *International Journal of Health Services*, 40: 1, pp. 97–117.

Atkinson, A. B. (2015). *Inequality, What Can Be Done?* Cambridge: Harvard University Press.

Baker, J., Lynch, K., Cantillion, S. and Walsh, J. (2004). *Equality: From Theory to Action*. Basingstoke: Palgrave Macmillan.

Baker, J., Lynch, K., Cantillion, S. and Walsh, J. (2009). *Equality: From Theory to Action: Second Edition*. Basingstoke: Palgrave Macmillan.

Barasch, I. M. (2005). *Desmond Tutu on compassion*, http://www.psychologytoday.com/articles/200504/desmond-tutu-compassion

Bessant, J. (2007). Not such a fair go: An audit of children's and young people's rights in Australia. *Scottish Youth Issues Journal*, 9, 41–56. Retrieved 15 February 2008 from http://www.youthlinkscotland.org/webs/245/documents/SYIJIss9.pdf

Blackburn, R. M. (2008). What is social inequality? *International Journal of Sociology and Social Policy*, 28, 7, pp. 250–59.

Burchardt, T. and Craig, G. (2008). Introduction. In G. Craig, T. Burchardt and D. Gordon, *Social Justice and Public Policy: Seeking Fairness in Diverse Societies*. Bristol: Policy Press.

Capeheart, L. and Milovanovic, D. (2007). *Social Justice: Theories, Issues, and Movements*. New Brunswick: Rutgers University Press.

Clark, D. A. (2006). The Capability Approach: Its development, critiques and recent advances. Global Poverty Research Group. ESRC. Retrieved 25 November, 2008, from http://economics.ouls.ox.ac.uk/14051/1/gprg-wps-032.pdf

Coburn, A. (2011). Liberation or containment: Paradoxes in youth work as a catalyst for powerful learning. *Journal of Youth and Policy*, 106, 66–77.

Coburn, A. and Gormally, S. (2015). Emancipatory praxis—A social justice approach to equality work. In C. Cooper, S. Gormally and G. Hughes, *Social Justice & Radical Alternatives for Education & Youth Work Practice: Re-imagining Ways of Working with Young People*. Basingstoke: Palgrave MacMillan.

Cooper, C., Gormally, S. and Hughes, G. (2015). *Social Justice & Radical Alternatives for Education & Youth Work Practice: Re-imagining Ways of Working with Young People*. Basingstoke: Palgrave MacMillan.

Corney, T. (2004). Value versus competencies: Implications for the future of professional youth work education. *Journal of Youth Studies*, 7(4), 513–527.

Crooks, M. (1992). Social justice: Core value of youth work. *Youth Issues Forum*, Spring, 20–24.

Craig, G. (2005). Delivering social justice through philanthropy http://www.alliancemagazine. org/feature/delivering-social-justice-through-philanthropy/, accessed on 1 May 2015.

Davies, B. (2005). Youth work: A manifesto for our times. *Journal of Youth and Policy*, 88, 1–23.

Deuchar, R. (2009). *Gangs, Marginalised Youth and Social Capital*. Stoke on Trent: Trentham.

Deuchar, R. and Maitles, H. (2008). Education for citizenship. In T. Bryce and W. Humes (Eds.), *Scottish Education: Beyond Devolution* (3rd ed., pp. 285–292). Edinburgh: Edinburgh University Press.

Dorling, D. (2013). Fairness and the changing fortunes of people in Britain. *Journal of the Royal Statistical Society*, 176: 1. (dannydorling.org).

Englund, T., Quennerstedt, A., and Wahlström, N. (2009). Education as a human and a citizenship right—Parents' rights, children's rights, or …? The necessity of historical contextualization. *Journal of Human Rights*, 8(2), 133–138.

European Commission. (2001). A new impetus for European youth. White Paper. Available at http://aei.pitt.edu/1186/1/youth_wp_COM_2001_681.pdf

Fernandez, F. (2000). Beyond the Capitalist Welfare State *LBJ Journal of Public Affairs*. Spring, 74–84. Retrieved September, 2008, from: http://www.lbjjournal.com/system/files/2000_annual_10_Beyond_the_Capitalist_Welfare_State.pdf

Fraser, N. (1997). *Justice Interruptus*. New York and London: Routledge.

Fraser, N. (2009). Social justice in the age of identity politics, redistribution, recognition and participation. In G. Henderson and M. Waterstone (Eds.), *Geographic Thought: A Praxis Perspective*. Oxon: Routledge.

Freire, P. (1970). *Pedagogy of the Oppressed*. New York: Penguin Books.

Fulcher, J. and Scott, J. (2007). *Sociology*. Oxford: Open University Press.

Giroux, H. A. (2005). *Border Crossings: Cultural Workers and the Politics of Education* (2nd Ed.). Oxon: Routledge Publishing.

Giroux, H. A. (2014). *Thinking Dangerously in an Age of Political Betrayal*. Truth-Out Retrieved 14 July from http://www.truth-out.org/opinion/item/24869-henry-a-giroux-thinking-dangerously-in-an-age-of-political-betrayal

Goodman, J. D. (2011). *Promoting Diversity and Social Justice: Educating People from Privileged Groups*, New York: Routledge.

Gormally, S. (2012). A social justice approach to community development. *The Irish Journal of Community Work*, Issue 3.

Hamilton, C. and Seymour, M. (2006). ASBOs and behaviour orders: Institutionalized intolerance of youth? *Youth Studies Ireland*, 1(1), 61–76.

Henriques, A. and Richardson, J. (Eds.) (2013). *The Triple Bottom Line, Does it All Add Up?* London: Routledge

Heywood, A. (2007). *Political Ideologies: An Introduction*, 4th Edition. Basingstoke: Basingstoke: Palgrave Macmillan.

Hughes, G., Cooper, C., Gormally, S. and Rippingale, J. (2014). The state of youth work in austerity England—Reclaiming the ability to 'care'. *Youth & Policy*, 113: 1–14.

Jeffs, T., and Smith, M. K. (Eds.) (2010). *Youth Work Practice*. Hampshire: Palgrave Macmillan.

Ledwith, M. and Springett, J. (2009). *Participatory Practice: Community-based Action for Transformative Change*. Bristol: Policy Press.

Lister, R. (2008). Recognition and voice: The challenge for social justice. In G. Craig, T. Burchardt and D. Gordon, *Social Justice and Public Policy: Seeking Fairness in Diverse Societies*. Bristol: Policy Press.

Meckled-Garcia, S. (2011). *Human rights or social justice? Rescuing human rights from the outcomes view*. London: UCL, School of Public Policy Working Paper Series: ISSN 1479–9472.

Merton et al. (2004). An Evaluation of the Impact of Youth Work in England. Youth Affairs Unit, University of DeMontfort, Nottingham, DfES Publications. Retrieved Sept 30th, 2016 from: http://webarchive.nationalarchives.gov.uk/20130323013919/https://www.education.gov.uk/publications/eOrderingDownload/RR606.pdf

McGinley, B. P. (2014). *Understanding Youth Work Law*. London: Sage.

Narayan, U. (2000). Essence of Culture and Sense of History: A Feminist Critique of Cultural Essentialism in Narayan, U and Harding, S. (eds.) *Decentering the Center: Philosophy for a Multicultural, Postcolonial, and Feminist World*, pp. 80–100. Bloomington: Indiana University Press.

Nussbaum, M. (1999). *Sex and Social Justice*, New York, Oxford University Press.

Nussbaum, M. C. (2003). Capabilities as fundamental entitlements: Sen and social justice. *Feminist Economics*, 9(2/3), 33–59.

Podd, W. (2010). Participation. In J. Batsleer and B. Davies (Eds.), *What Is Youth Work?* (pp. 20–32). Exeter: Learning Matters.

Rawls, J. (1971). *A Theory of Justice*. Cambridge: Harvard University Press.

Rawls, J. (2001). *Justice as Fairness: A Restatement*. Cambridge: Harvard University Press.

Rudnick, A., Montgomery, P., Coatsworth-Puspoky, R., Cohen, B., Forchuk, C., Lahey, P., Perry, S. and Schofield, R. Perspectives of social justice among people living with mental illness and poverty: A qualitative study. (2014). *Journal of Poverty and Social Justice*, Vol. 22: 2, pp. 147–57.

Ruesga, A. G. and Puntenney, D. (2010). *Social Justice Philanthropy: An Initial Framework for Positioning this Work*. Philanthropy for Social Justice and Peace.

Scottish Executive. (2007). Moving forward: A strategy for improving young people's chances through youth work. One Scotland. Retrieved 29 May 2017 from http://www.gov.scot/Resource/Doc/169328/0047167.pdf

Scullion, G. (2011). In K. Healey and M. O'Prey (Eds.), *Taking a Social Justice Approach to Community Development: A New Support and Development Model for Local Community Groups*, Belfast: Community Foundation for Northern Ireland.

Sen, A. (1985). Well-being, agency and freedom: The Dewey lectures 1984. *Journal of Philosophy 82*, 169–221. Retrieved 10 May 2010 from http://www.freelogy.org/w/images/d/dc/Sen85.pdf

Sen, A. (2009). *On Justice*. London: Palgrave.

Shaw, M. and McCulloch, K. (2009). Hooligans or rebels? Thinking more critically about citizenship and young people. *Journal of Youth and Policy*, 101, pp. 5–14.

Smith, M. K. (2002). Youth work: An introduction. *The Encyclopaedia of Informal Education*. Retrieved 24 May 2007 from www.infed.org/youthwork/b-yw.htm

Taylor, T. (2010). Defending democratic youth work. *Concept, 1*(2), 3–10.

Tawney, H. R. (1964). *Equality*. London: Allen and Unwin.

Thompson, N. (1997) *Anti-discriminatory Practice* (2nd Ed.). Basingstoke: MacMillan.

Thompson, N. (2003). *Promoting Equality: Challenging Discrimination and Oppression* (2nd Ed.). Basingstoke: Palgrave MacMillan.

United Nations (1948). *Declaration of Human Rights*. Retrieved October 10, 2010, from URL: "http://un.org/en/%20documents/udhr" www.un.org/en/ documents/udhr

United Nations (1989). *United Nations Convention on the Rights of the Child*, (UNCROC) Adopted by the General Assembly of the United Nations, 20th November, 2014.

Wilkinson, R. and Pickett, K. (2010). *The Spirit Level: Why Equality Is Better for Everyone*, London: Penguin Books.

Young, I. M. (1990). *Justice and the Politics of Difference*. Oxford: Princeton University Press.

Young, K. (2006). *The Art of Youth Work* (2nd Ed.). Lyme Regis: Russell House Publishing.

Young, I. M. (2008). Structural injustice and the politics of difference. In G. Craig, T. Burchardt and D. Gordon, *Social Justice and Public Policy: Seeking Fairness in Diverse Societies*. Bristol: Policy Press.

· 4 ·

COMMUNITY

Introduction

This chapter discusses what is meant by community as the context for community practitioners working with people to advance the cause of social justice and equality. It explores the nature and purpose of community as a means of creating identity and cohesion (Cohen 1985; Delanty, 2005) among people who define boundaries in order to make sense of their world. The impact of globalisation and the market with its links to social capital are also critiqued. The chapter uses bricolage as a frame for unifying early and contemporary constructions of community as a system for connectedness and cohesion. This shows that community takes differing forms, including geographical or physical spaces, on-line or virtual communities, and community as social practices (Delanty, 2009; Ledwith, 2011; Shaw and Crowther, 2013; Wenger, 1998).

Back to the Future?

According to Blackshaw (2010, p. 204), 'Community matters to neoliberals because it sells'. The idea of community as a prefix to health, housing, policing or regeneration invokes feelings of goodness and fits with a cultural narrative of belonging and social cohesion. Drawing on Durkheim, Blackshaw asserts that this is because historic constructions of community have identified that it is developed through social ties that help to bond people together as an integrating force. Blackshaw (2010) also suggests that while the idea of community has been described as something that should be nurtured and cherished, 'much empirical work has overstated the significance of social relationships and social solidarity' (p. 9).

Community is perceived as a safety device that allows people to sleep easy at night—exemplified in the emergence of walled or gated communities, where people of a certain age or social disposition connect together for their improved sense of security. Yet, the shift from industrial to technological; from local to global markets; from social democracy to neoliberalism have created so many variables in constructing a theory of community that it is at best, contested and at worst, so fluid it has become meaningless to many. In order to understand why perspectives on community are changing, we need to consider how previous constructions of community have influenced, and been influenced by, the development of the social world.

Early constructions of community were created at micro or macro levels, around physical spaces or locations (the village or the neighbourhood) or were often grouped around particular interests or specific aspects such as race, religion or social class. Tonnies in the nineteenth century was interested in the conflicting tensions in historical and rational perspectives on community and civil society. Tonnies offered explanation on the basis of Gemeinschaft—where 'community' offers a traditional and tangible reality for social relations in terms of association with others in a locality, in folklore or through religious belief, and Gesellshcaft—where 'society' offers an imagined structure for social relations in terms of conventional wisdom, legislation and public opinion (Delanty, 2003). Theorising community and society in this way could be viewed as a polarisation of social life, a duality of actual and more elusive structures.

Yet, Tonnies (1887) suggested that, although different, both community and society offered a way of thinking about living in association with others, and according to Delanty (2003) in pursuit of 'a more radical form of socialism … as natural to society as individualism' (p. 33–34). Tonnies' work is critiqued, for example in asserting the importance of shared membership of networks as a source of solidarity, Putnam (2000) argues these as more useful in achieving social connectedness and building capacity for social action, than traditional values of family and kinship ties. This critique persists in Giddens'

(2003) perspectives on how social change and in particular the processes of globalisation have impacted on everyday lived experiences. In this way, any explanation of community as a romantic throwback to the kind of village life encountered in traditional rural communities is largely redundant in offering a simplistic response to the kind of alienation experienced by people, in an industrial and internet connected society.

In conceptualising community, the idea of alienation alerts us to the importance of social connection. Alienation was proposed by Marx (1990) in his explanation of inequalities of social class within a capitalist system that reduces the individual to a commodity, through the objectification of their labour, in order to sustain unequal power relations. Thus, according to Marx, individual labour is paid for as a commodity by those who control or monopolise the market, and who profit from the labour of people who are often many steps removed the site of production. Reid (1972) suggested alienation as, 'the frustration of ordinary people excluded from the processes of decision making. The feeling of hopelessness that pervades people who feel, with justification, that they have no real say in shaping or determining their own destiny' (p. 5).

The concept of alienation offers a context for learning in community development work that interrogates the complex problems that underpin contemporary persistence in pathologising certain behaviours as antisocial while also dehumanising people to the point of ruthlessness and a self-serving grasping of power. This raises questions on why people are excluded from decision making, how this pathology persists in de-socialising those who are identified as anti-social, and in analysing power relations in order to facilitate community and individual empowerment.

Such questions make critical pedagogy possible in helping to ensure that, 'People are more likely to become involved if they are less alienated from decision-making structures' (Gunn, 2006, p. 26). As a starting point for community work with people who seek to challenge inequality, problem posing can create dialogue for production of a counter-hegemony that promotes a moral and ethical construction of what it means to be human, and what kind of social relationships are helpful in promoting equality and social justice.

Yet, in seeking to engage people who have been most severely impacted by poverty, alienation and inequality, community participation can also be problematic. In places where education is introduced, for example as an 'intervention', 'problem-solving initiative' or 'diversion from crime' this impact on the possibility of authentic participation where, 'in reality, "problem" communities of the poor are increasingly targeted for attention in ways which make participation potentially an instrument of therapy or indeed surveillance' (Shaw, Meagher and Moir, 2006, p. 11). In planning to work with communities for social change, it is thus important to consider not only a range of types of community but also to consider the impact of neoliberal capitalism on those various communities, in order to understand how the prevailing hegemony might be challenged.

One popular theory that has taken hold is social capital. Despite being aligned to capitalism in its use of language and in offering an alternative yet, similarly hierarchical, means of creating social order we are interested in the extent to which alternative capitals, developed around social and cultural relationships, might offer an antidote to the 'unbridled individualism' (Field, 2003, p. 7) of the Reagan/Thatcher legacy. It is important to be fully conscious of the inherent possibilities for social capital to be used in creating and sustaining inequality, for example in peoples' use of networks and connections to advance their own interests, or in the trading of human capital as a commodity in the market place. However, the concept also brings into focus the ways that people form social relationships to create solidarity and so offers insights that help us to understand the nature, purpose and potential of community as a useful way of enhancing cohesion.

Social and Cultural Capitals

The concept of social capital was largely developed through the work of three key theorists (Coleman 1988, Bourdieu 1991, Putnam 2000). Bourdieu (1991) developed a cultural anthropological theory of social reproduction and was interested in the persistence of social class and other forms of inequality. Coleman (1988) was also interested in inequality but focused on how social capital might explain differences in academic achievement.

Taking a broader view, Bourdieu (1991) considered how groups used cultural symbols to signify and mark their position within social structures. Bourdieu's conceptualisation of habitus is helpful in discussion of community. It suggests a structured set of values or ways of thinking that provide a bridge between different kinds of community, whereby localised habitus, its value base and social structures, can either encourage or discourage participation in the community, where loose ties might be developed and boundaries crossed in order to form different kinds of relationships. Putnam (2000) and Woolcock

(1998) described two types of social capital: bonding capital (exclusive) or bridging capital (inclusive).

Bonding capital holds people together and helps maintain in-group loyalty by reinforcing specific identities and mobilising solidarity, while bridging capital works across social divisions and connects people to external assets, beyond the immediate family. A social capital frame suggests that, by bringing people together, community workers create conditions for bonding, and to a lesser extent, bridging capitals by offering a place to meet and by posing problems that promote dialogue and in doing so, potentially builds community cohesion.

Putnam (2000) was enthusiastic for volunteering and socialising or associating with others as a means of countering corporate power and social apathy. Rejecting Tonnies (1887) dualism, Putnam argued that rather than kinship, secondary associations were more useful in connecting people. While this goes some way towards creating an alternative to corporate power, with its discourse that is directly linked to the hegemonic language of capitalism, social capital thus offers a flawed paradigm for social change. For example, the appropriation of social and cultural capitals to substantiate a single view of people as tightly bonded, homogenous groups, in terms of age, gender, race or religion. However, in the world that we currently occupy, it is at least useful to consider alternative forms of capital that strengthen capability for the continued evolution of the democracy project.

Bourdieu's (1991) ideas on social capital as part of cultural capital, suggest social capital as inextricably linked to the cultural context of peoples' lives. The need to acquire and understand cultural capital thus becomes an intrinsic part of how people use social and other capitals. This takes a slightly different view to literature that argues for social capital to be regarded as a mobilising agent for other capitals (Bassani 2007). Instead, we suggest that mobilising capital is linked to both social and cultural capitals and to the connections people make through community practices. These two capitals go hand in hand, for example, in crossing boundaries between social friendship and cultural projects or in relationships that are formed on-line and bring the potential to reach across cultures or established social groups. Thus, the distinction between social and cultural capitals appears blurred and suggests that bridging capital does not in itself cause capital to increase, rather 'it provides the group with resources that can be mobilized' (Bassani, 2007, p. 29).

In empirical research about how young people learned about equality (Coburn 2012), two youth exchange groups involved in both hosting and visiting each other, engaged in dialogue about what it meant to be young and living in different social and cultural circumstances. The findings suggested that they built relationships across cultural boundaries, which helped to increase their awareness of difference and of themselves. Cohen (1985) proposed that, in order to value their own culture, people need to stand at the boundary between what is considered normal, and what contradicts normality, in order to become self-aware. Of particular relevance to this discussion of social and cultural capital, the above study showed that young people formed a series of relationships that were developed and negotiated over time (Coburn, 2012). The changing nature of these relationships suggested that simply attending the youth project and engaging in pleasantries with youth workers would not in itself lead to an accumulation of positive social capital or to learning about what it means to be a social being. Findings identified that short term participation would not have brought the required investments in time, commitment or obligation that are suggested by Putnam (2000) as important to development of an ongoing project that would help to build and sustain social relationships. Yet, this study identified that over time, and by forming relationships across social and cultural boundaries, participants were able to see and understand different perspectives and so revise their previously held views on difference.

Thus, in youth and community work, just as it was with Putnam's metaphor of league bowlers, it is important to have 'regular participation with a diverse set of acquaintances ... [to] ... represent a form of sustained social capital that is not matched by an occasional pick-up game' (Putnam, 2000, p. 113), in order to negotiate a series of changing educational relationships. This longer-term engagement is noted as important in thinking about communities as environments for learning (Gilchrist and Taylor, 2001) where, 'shared values ... [are] ... as important to people's experience of community as shared living space ... [where] ... networks ... provide an important vehicle for collective learning and the accumulation of cultural memories and local knowledge' (p. 108). Being part of community enables people to stand at the boundary of that community, aware of their own culture but also able to see other cultures as similar or different to themselves. In this sense, being part of a community can be seen as a means of identity formation, where the role of the community practitioner is to:

'... support people in developing and expressing their own identities, if necessary in opposition to those that have been thrust upon them by the existing economic and social order'.

Shaw (2013, p. 8)

When people are connected by a shared or common identity, or when they interact with each other in a particular or systematic way, they can identify as a social group. Members of a social group share the privileges or disadvantages that come with belonging to the group. They also share, or work together, to create histories, values and purposes that can define them as a community of interest or identity (Willmott, 1986), which is important in challenging inequality and oppression.

Yet, ideas on identity and community are shifting in an ever-changing world of globalisation and consumerist market forces. Beck (1992) conceptualised increasing risk as a consequence of globalisation, where there was a shift from the political and economic structures of the industrial age, which were largely concerned with class struggle, to the ecological risks associated with rapid technological and scientific advances. According to Beck, these advances bring uncertainty and a new set of risks for people to manage. In turn, the feelings of uncertainty that come from having to manage a range of new risks add even more uncertainty, which heightens people's anxiousness about risk.

In particular, Beck (1992) suggested that while the basis of class struggle during the industrial age was well established in issues of poverty and inequality, the nature of risks in modern society was untested and unclear. The lack of clarity and the pace of change, for Beck, suggested the importance of individual judgements in constructing a future where people need to take risks into account when judging whether or not to engage in a particular course of action. This has contributed to increased individualisation of the processes through which people make sense of the world and emphasises the importance of the individual in determining their own futures. This individualised understanding of the social world clearly has an impact on exploring community. If our focus is on community risk rather than community cohesion, how does this inform perspectives on what community means, what it is and what it means to connect with people, who are inside or outside of a particular community?

Bauman (2000; 2012) has described this current 'risky' period as one of 'liquid modernity'. Bauman uses this term to define a time when people live with so much uncertainty that the concept of community helps them to find roots in an otherwise precarious existence. The concept is unrecognisable in terms of its former purpose in sustaining social connectivity through symbols and localised contractual obligations and relationships. Instead, the nature of community is more tenuous and fragmented than ever before, and yet, there is an 'unstoppably rising volume of "uprooted" people - migrants, refugees, exiles, asylum seekers: people on the move and without permanent abode' (Bauman, 2012, Foreward, p. ix). Bauman also offers hope in conceptualising networked communities that are created through human interactions among individuals whose identities are formed in advance of their engagement within a particular community, not because of it. In this sense, a community is sustained because individual people believe it to be important. This has utility for community practices that are aligned to social movements for change, in connecting people around a particular cause or interest.

Yet, networks alone do not explain the persistence of community which, according to Delanty, 'consists in its ability to communicate ways of belonging, especially in the context of an increasingly insecure world' (2005, p. 187). While we are sceptical about its use as a woolly security blanket, the idea of community as a means of communicating ways of belonging, suggests that it is a useful concept for bringing people together in order to develop new ways of knowing and understanding. As the context for youth and community work, it is useful for practitioners to be aware of how participation can be sustained by strengthening the connections people make with each other, so that, even where they are loosely coupled and not so tightly knit as in the past, communities can still connect people and facilitate the kind of collective solidarity that underpins social change.

Although these localised or interest driven communities persist, new kinds of community have also emerged. So, in addition to people connecting together in geographic communities or around particular interests, there are also new forms of community that are constructed differently through social media or as social practices. These new communities use on-line environments to connect both locally and internationally. This multiplicity of community makes it difficult to understand what it means as the context for community work that advances the cause of social justice and equality. Such communities not only work independently of each other but can also be connected and overlapping in helping people to form or affirm identity, to make sense or meaning of the world, and to become resilient to the world we currently occupy. Thinking about the complexities and distinctions in how communities are created and strengthened, makes the task of a single or even dual conceptualisation of community impossible. Shaw (2013) takes this argument further by suggesting that:

'... competing visions of community have consistently jostled for authority within professional discourses ... [and] ... the tension between 'the community' singular, as an expression of inclusion and solidarity, and 'communities' plural, as a potentially exclusive experience of difference, is central to an understanding of the complex relationship between theory and practice in community work'.

Shaw (2013, p. 2)

This level of complexity and competing visions of community, has led us to the concept of bricolage, as a useful means of synthesising discussion and conceptualising disparate types of community, especially when traditional ideas have changed so much in the last few decades.

Bricolage is already recognised as useful in conceptualising multidisciplinary and diverse research methods (Denzin and Lincoln, 2000; Kincheloe, 2001; 2005) and as a means to 'criticalize and rigourize the traditional ways in which to do multi-methodological research' Steinberg (2011, p. 176). The French word bricolage is defined as making something or putting something together using whatever materials are available. It is used in architecture to denote the effect of close proximity in buildings from different periods or different architectural styles. According to Rogers, (2012) 'Bricolage addresses the plurality and complex political dimensions of knowledge work' (p. 14) and as such could be applied, not only in research contexts, but also in seeking to extend knowledge and understanding of complex ideas such as community. In conceptualising community as bricolage, we bring together old and new ideas in order to understand each of the four different kinds of community as they are constructed and contextualised in different time-periods and in different ways or contexts. The concept of bricolage is useful in drawing together old, new and as yet unimagined forms of community in local and global communities (real or virtual) without privileging one form over another. The remainder of this chapter outlines different types of community that can be a useful starting point for development of emancipatory praxis. These combine to form our 'bricolage' of community as: physical, virtual and social.

Community as Physical Space

The idea of community as physical space is not new. For centuries, people would meet family, make friends and connect with each other in their local geographical area and this underpinned human existence in creating a sense of belonging, and feelings of connection and of being safe and secure. The industrial revolution brought a physical shift from rural to urban lifestyles where people lived and worked in localised physical communities, and the idea of community served those same needs for belonging, connection and safety. The physical community underpinned social and familial relationships that were boundaried by place in, for example, the geography of a mining village built around the pit or a terraced row where whole families lived within three streets of each other and worked in the same factory. This created a utopian view of family and community, where everyone knew each other's business and families saw each other every day. According to Ritzer (2008) Weber's conceptualisation of an ideal or utopian type, was not meant as the 'best of all possible worlds' (p. 121) but could be described in static or dynamic contexts.

The shift from heavy industry towards a knowledge and leisure based economy has fragmented families as, according to Giddens (2003), work patterns have changed, to include people relocating to find suitable employment or short-term projects and flexible hours working. People still live in physical spaces, in terms of housing and social amenities and most can name a physical community that they call home (in the sense that they feel it is a place where they belong, or at least is a place they occupy on a regular basis). However, an impact of globalisation has meant that, 'Community, labour and capital are increasingly placeless' (Ritzer, 2008, p. 557).

Routinely, public services and amenities are organised around a physical community but this kind of community is not the cohesive unit it once was. People are familiar with churches, mosques, shopping centres, schools and clubs as places they visit or pass regularly, which underpins their sense of belonging to that particular community. However, the decline, for some, of close proximity extended families and an increase in living among neighbours who hardly know each other, means that this feeling of belonging can relate more to a geographical space than to any kind of social connectedness. Yet, the idea of community still seems to project a positive construction which remains pervasive in the quest for a sense of belonging (Putnam, 2000).

So, although physical community cannot be recognised in the same way as it was before, the idea of being part of and participating in, a physical community remains useful. Arguably, people still utilise the amenities in the physical locality through going to the local school to see their children's play, participation in local clubs and socialising at the local pub. This is particularly the case when faced with a problem or changing circumstances such as high levels of unemployment or proposals to relocate a local school. Such localised problems can act as a catalyst for bringing people together, to work with each other in order to influence decisions and resolve problems, '… by drawing on the power of the community rather than simply individual effort' (Heywood, 2007, p. 102). This shifts the physical community towards an interest community. As people focus on the problem they find a common interest and in doing so form bonds that help them build a cohesive response to aspirations and needs. This bond develops over time to strengthen relationships of solidarity.

Community as Virtual Environment

The idea of community as virtual environment is fairly new, the world wide web was invented in 1989 and since then the virtual environment has burgeoned as a means of learning about 'everything', listening to music, meeting people, ordering food, playing games, sharing family photos, saying good night to grandkids, socializing, working … living! Understanding community in this new virtual world can be a powerful tool in promoting equality and social justice. While there are changes in the nature of traditional communities, described by Turner (2001) as thick or organic, the internet has opened up possibilities for creation of new kinds of on-line community. Turner suggests these types of communities can be described as thin, comprising strangers in a virtual world, where change happens fast and where the power of the post can put the pen into oblivion.

Like the web itself, community as virtual environment is not fully developed but it is interesting to note that physical communities are replicated on-line either as simulation games or as real places, e.g., on member-only Facebook pages where people from across the planet can reconnect, for example, with their former home or school community. While there is a view of virtual community that is argued as, 'more than a compensation for the real world it is an escape from the real world' Delanty (2003, p. 174) it is also suggested that, 'virtual communities can support existing relations but rarely create new ones, except those that require the sharing of information … [and may be described as] … networks of sociability' Delanty (2003, p. 177). Building on the idea of community as accessible space, outside of the 'real' world but able to be accessed, and as a space for information sharing across networks of sociability; we propose that a virtual environment does therefore create possibilities for new kinds of community that may be short term but can be effective in connecting and informing people that enables them to take action for social change. This kind of short-term response can be exemplified in the way that social media can be used to show solidarity with a particular cause or to create an immediate link to a petition that calls for Government action.

Community as Social Practice

In theorising community of practice, Wenger (1998) suggests that social practice is concerned with the everyday activities that facilitate a sharing of resources and underpin specific ways of engaging with the world (p. 13). Identity is about the social formation of the person and the complex range of markers that differentiate individuals (p. 13). Wenger also identified characteristics of a community of practice as mutual engagement, joint enterprise and shared repertoire (p. 73). Yet, the world is not fixed and people are guided by different ideas or beliefs, or live in different cultural and social circumstances. This creates boundaries and borders between people and practices that are socially constructed through processes of making meaning and acts of being. Wenger called this dual product/process as reification (1998, p. 59). Considering boundaries as reification shows them as socially constructed products that can also be the process through which they are socially deconstructed. Deconstructing boundaries and borders involves working within and outside of current discourse to create new ideas or alternative forms of knowledge (Giroux, 2005). In this sense, working on the boundaries of communities, and seeing community as social practice could also be regarded as one of mutual interest, where joint enterprise and shared values or beliefs can strengthen connections and build relationships as both products and processes of practice.

Wenger also suggests that negotiation of meaning and understanding are shaped by time and place, by physical environment, by social relationships and by the individual or collective ideas of those involved whereby the evolution of social practices is achieved through a mutual alignment of 'repertoire, styles and discourses' (Wenger, 1998, p. 95). Seeing community in this way is useful on two levels. First, community as social practice can assist in understanding the practitioner as a member of a particular practice community, which offers affirmation, a sense of belonging and continuity. Second, community as social practice can assist in understanding how practice is developed by practitioners working together with members of geographic and virtual communities who are working together and engaged in mutual alignment with the repertoire, styles and discourses of a particular practice community. This offers possibilities for new ways of crafting community work practice to advance the causes of equality and social justice.

For example, adult educators operate at the boundaries of practice across areas such as adult learning, employability, health improvement and literacy. This helps them to affirm specific practices and also to work across borders to build new ideas and perspectives. In doing so, the adult educator is able to engage across different communities of practice, by crossing disciplinary boundaries in health and literacy while maintaining a strong professional identity that is both affirmed by, and affirming of, adult education practice. Wenger calls this affirmation and consolidation of practice a 'duality of boundary relations' (Wenger, 1998, p. 104).

Considering Community as a Bricolage

Theorising physical, virtual and social practice communities as having the capability to support development of a duality of community relations, we propose that all three kinds of community are important aspects of emancipatory praxis because they each work to affirm community practice and to consolidate what this practice does. First, community as physical space/ place is proposed as important in framing practice processes in youth work, community development and adult education and in strengthening local ties that help to create a response to local inequalities and enhance social cohesion. Second, community as a virtual environment is proposed as a useful process for connecting people at micro and macro levels in order to challenge inequalities and to promote social change through production of improved connection and solidarity. Thirdly, as social practice, community is proposed as an ethical means of promoting equality and social justice, where community practitioners can coalesce around a community of practice that offers a sense of belonging and a safe space for self-care and professional development.

In producing a bricolage of useful but distinctly different communities, in regard to their nature and purpose, we assert that community is indeed a fluid and multi-variant concept that comprises different constituent parts, some of which are still evolving and all of which can serve specific interests or commonalities. Rather than reject these distinctions as unhelpful, we find that this reflects the changing shape and nature of communities. It responds to the ways in which communities are created within a technologically advancing society that also remains blighted by poverty, discrimination and

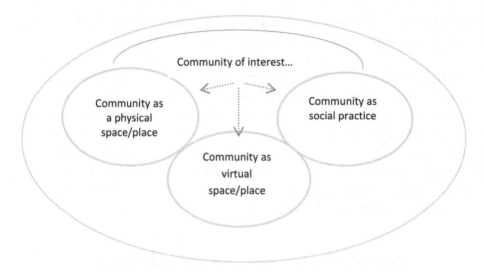

Figure 3. A Bricolage of Community.

inequality. We believe that all parts of this bricolage of community bring possibilities for social change wherever and however inequality and social injustice prevails.

As practitioners, we assert that a fusion of conceptualisations of community is especially useful as it opens up possibilities for new social practices and for the reification of community, which Wenger (1998) asserts as a 'process of giving form to our experience by producing objects that congeal this experience into "thingness" … around which the negotiation of meaning becomes organised' (p. 58). This conceptualisation reaches a wide range of people by maximising use of local and global networks to create a hybrid of distinctions that are connected, and can also be used to achieve connection, in different ways in order to achieve a common purpose. We assert this reification of community on all levels identified and those still to be developed, as an effective means of facilitating social change. At a local level, community offers a route into 'political education and social action focused on concrete issues and concerns' (Martin, 1987, p. 200) which means that, 'practice grows out of the social and political experiences of people in communities and attempts to forge a direct link between education and social action' (Tett, 2010, p. 29). Our construction of community as bricolage offers a means of connecting people in order to challenge the prevailing forces of materialist capitalism that seek to pathologise and stigmatise the poor through aggressive structures of corporate power.

Conclusion

In recognising the contested and fluid nature of community, we remain convinced of its utility in connecting people to bring about social change. Rather than rejecting current interpretations of romanticised community or in overstating solidarity as inherently characteristic of community, we propose that despite or perhaps even because of Bauman's idea of liquid modernity (2000; 2012), the concept persists in different forms as a touchstone for the animation of people and praxis in working together for the common good. In this way, people can work together for and with each other in order to change their social world. Community can thus be considered as a catalyst for political and social action. Having identified usefulness in community as a multi-variant and connecting concept in bringing about social change, we now go on to analyse power and to consider contexts in which community empowerment might be achieved through community practice.

Bibliography

Bassani, C. (2007). Five dimensions of social capital theory as they pertain to youth studies. *Journal of Youth Studies*, 10(1), 17–34.

Bauman, Z. (2012). *Liquid Modernity*. (2nd Ed.). Cambridge: Polity Press with Oxford: Blackwell.

Bauman, Z. (2000). *Liquid Modernity*. Cambridge: Polity Press with Oxford: Blackwell.

Beck, U. (1992). *Risk Society: Towards a New Modernity* (Translated by Rutter, M.). London: Sage.

Blackshaw, T. (2010). *Key Concepts in Community Studies*. London, Sage.

Bourdieu, P. (1991). *Language and Symbolic Power*. Cambridge: Polity Blackwell.

Coburn, A. (2012). Learning about equality: A study of a generic youth work setting. Unpublished thesis. Glasgow: University of Strathclyde.

Cohen, A. P. (1985). *The Symbolic Construction of Community*. London: Routledge.

Coleman, J. C. (1988). Social capital in the creation of human capital. *American Journal of Sociology*, 94, S95–S120.

Delanty, G. (2003). *Community*. London: Routledge.

Denzin, N. and Lincoln, Y. (2000). The discipline and practice of qualitative research. In N. Denzin and Y. Lincoln (Eds.), *Handbook of Qualitative Research* (3rd Ed., pp. 1–28) Thousand Oaks: Sage.

Field, J. (2003). *Social Capital*. London: Routledge.

Giddens, A. (2003). *Sociology* (4th Ed.). Cambridge: Polity Press.

Gilchrist, A. and Taylor, M. (2011). *The Short Guide to Community Development*. Bristol: Policy Press.

Giroux, H. (2005). *Border crossings*. Oxon: Routledge.

Heywood, A. (2007). *Political Ideologies: An Introduction*, 4th Edition. Basingstoke: Basingstoke: Palgrave Macmillan.

Kincheloe, J. (2001). Describing the bricolage: Conceptualizing a new rigor in qualitative research. *Qualitative Inquiry*. 7(6), 679–692.

Kincheloe, J. (2005). On to the next level: Continuing the conceptualization of the bricolage. *Qualitative Inquiry*. Sage 323–350.

Ledwith, M. (2011). *Community Development: A Critical Approach*. Bristol: The Policy Press.

Marx, K. (1990) *Capital: Critique of Political Economy V1*, Ben Fowkes (Translator), London: Penguin Classics.

Martin, I. (1987). Community Education: towards a theoretical analysis in R, Edwards., S, Sieminski., D, Zeldin. (Eds) *Adult Learners, Education, and Training: A Reader*, London: Open University.

Putnam, R. D. (2000). *Bowling Alone: The Collapse and Revival of American Community*. New York: Simon and Schuster.

Reid, J. (1972). *Alienation*. Rectorial address delivered in the University of Glasgow, April 1972.

Ritzer, G. (2008). Classical Sociological Theory (5th edition), New York, McGraw-Hill.

Rogers, M. (2008) Contextualising Theories and Practices of Bricolage Research. *The Qualitative Report*. 17(48), 1–17 Retrieved, 10 October 2016 from: http://nsuworks.nova.edu/tqr/vol17/iss48/3/

Shaw, M. and Crowther, J. (2014). Adult education, community development and democracy: Renegotiating the terms of engagement. *Community Development Journal*. Oxford: Oxford University Press. 49(3), 390–406

Shaw, M. (2013). Community work today: Competing demands in practice. *Concept*, 4(2). Edinburgh: University of Edinburgh. Accessed on 10 October 2015 at http://concept.lib.ed.ac.uk/index.php/Concept/article/view/220

Shaw, M., Meagher, J. and Moir, S. (2006). *Participation in community development: Problems and possibilities*. Edinburgh: University of Edinburgh.

Steinberg, S. (2011). *Kind erculture: The Corporate Construction of Childhood*. (3rd edition) Boulder, Colorado, Westview Press.

Tett, L. (2010). *Community Learning and Development* (3rd edition). Edinburgh: Dunedin Academic Press.

Turner B. S. (2001). The Erosion of Citizenship. *The Journal of Sociology*. 52(2), 189–209. Retrieved, 30th May 2015 from: http://onlinelibrary.wiley.com/doi/10.1080/00071310120044944/full

Wenger, E. (1998). *Communities of Practice: Learning, Meaning and Identity*. Cambridge: Cambridge University Press.

Willmott, P. (1986). *Social Networks, Informal Care and Public Policy*. London: Policy Studies Institute.

Woolcock, M. (1998). Social capital and economic development: Toward a theoretical synthesis and policy framework. *Theory and Society*, 27(2), 151–208.

· 5 ·

UNDERSTANDING POWER AND EMPOWERMENT

Introduction

This chapter explores the theoretical concepts of power and empowerment and questions how these relate to youth and community work. It analyses the resistance of power through community activism and the restrictors of power through gatekeeping. It argues that as community workers, we are engaging in constructed interactions that should not replicate nor promote power imbalances, but rather should be reflected upon and critiqued, in order to enhance positive social action. Youth work is concerned with 'tipping the balances of power in young people's favour' (Davies, 2005, p. 10) and developing power relationships that are enshrined in personal and social rights and are influenced by economically and politically dominant groups (Baker et al., 2004). Viewing power positively offers fluidity and promotes facilitation of an environment that enables or encourages power sharing as a critical part of a process that is complex, relational and situational. It suggests power can be a process which encourages a negotiated dialogue and a problem posing approach to learning (Freire, 1996). Foregrounding the kind of youth work and community development values and practices discussed in Chapter 2, the inherent power imbalances that are present in all practitioner relationships may also be reduced and as such, these values and practices create real opportunities for shifting power relations and developing progressive collaborative working practices.

Power

Power is a debated concept, as is the practical use of it and often empowerment is discussed as an aim of practice. Yet, empowerment cannot be effectively discussed or achieved before a thorough analysis of power is used to facilitate deeper knowledge and understanding of how power operates within relationships of oppression. As Foucault asserts:

> For me power is what needs to be explained ... That is, those facts of power, those power mechanisms, those power relations at work in the problem of madness, of medicine, of prison and so on. I have been trying to grapple with that bundle of empirical and poorly elucidated things which power relations consist of, taking them as something that needs explaining.
>
> Foucault (in Fabion, 2002, p. 284)

Lukes (1974) discusses various levels of power yet maintains a negatively focussed interpretation of the concept. Western social and political theorists traditionally focussed on power as domination, coercion or competition, at its best (Karlberg, 2005). In articulating power Lukes (1974) defined three main dimensions—direct, indirect and invisible; all of which were focussed on the negativity power can bring, with an emphasis on the domination of one person over another. In analysing power through a lens of domination, there is an assumption that those not wielding such power are 'victims'. This is clearly too simplistic and ignores the intrinsic power networks prevalent throughout society. Lukes (2004) does later criticise his original work acknowledging that his earlier proclamations:

> ... offers a very partial and one-sided account of the topic ... it focuses entirely on the exercise of power and ... it deals only with asymmetric power—the power of some *over* others.
>
> Lukes (2004, p. 64)

Alternatively, Morriss (2006) notes a different perspective where; 'Power' is best thought of as the ability to affect outcomes, not the ability to affect others' (Morriss, 2006, p. 126). This analysis provides a more positive outlook, providing a capacity to act autonomously to achieve change. Morriss (2006) similarly contextualises power in three ways: (1) practical—knowledge of our own power and that of others, (2) moral—the responsibility of having power, and (3) evaluative—evaluating the power of social systems. Discussing the difference between power-over and power-to, Morriss (2006) explains that individuals can have the power to carry out actions without having an underlying desire to dominate. This provides insight into the differing forms of power and suggests that power may be viewed as a capacity that does not have to be used negatively. Nevertheless, this does not eradicate the potential for power to be used in a negative or oppressive manner and Foucault's (1972) proposal that power is widespread throughout every social, economic and political relationship holds relevance for CYW practice.

Foucault (1972) was interested in establishing 'how' power is exercised and argued that power could only be asserted over 'free subjects' in a more subtle manner. In this way the production of knowledge is intrinsically linked to the exercise of power whereby institutions and systems, such as prisons, schools, etc., produce 'coherent systems of knowledge' and thus validate power (Ball, 2013, p. 13):

> ... If power is in reality an open, more-or-less coordinated (in the event, no doubt, ill-coordinated) cluster of relations, then the only problem is to provide oneself with a gird of analysis which makes possible an analytic of relations of power.
>
> Foucault (1980, p. 199)

These relations of power occur between everyone, as individuals, groups, institutions or communities. As such, a central theme of this work is that power is not possessed but rather it is exercised. Foucault (1980) suggested that power is not one dimensional but can be exercised in a number of formats. Further, power relations are intentional and where there is power, Foucault argues, there is resistance (Foucault, 1988). He saw the exercise of power as having potential for both enablement and constraint as opposed to solely a negative interpretation of power:

> Power is not a mode of subjugation, or a general system of domination and indeed power is as much about what can be said and thought as what can be done—it is discursive.
>
> Ball (2013, p. 30)

This makes us active participants in power relations and as practitioners and citizens it is important to have an awareness of these 'microphysics of power'

(Foucault, 1975) which means we should not only focus on sovereign or cen-tralized power. When working within the youth and community development field, Foucault's recognition of micro processes of power, as articulated in everyday conversation or in routine community activity, is as important as the larger, macro power analysis.

Analysing power as a 'capacity' demonstrated a movement from tradi-tional negative concepts of power (Karlberg, 2005) that is 'done to' people and creates possibilities for utilising power as a means to promote societal change or to enhance a 'transformative capacity' (Giddens, 1987) to change society.

Hunjan and Keophilavong (2010) identified three theoretical concep-tions of how power operates in practice:

"power to": individual ability to act	Citizen education and leadership devel-opment is rooted in the belief that every individual has the power to make a difference.
"power with": collective action, the ability to act together	Power with helps build bridges across different interests, experiences and knowledge.
"power within": individual or collective sense of self-worth, value, dignity	Increasing the power within individuals builds their capacities to imagine and raise aspirations about change.

Figure 4. Conceptualizations of Power.

Although useful, this needs to be understood in relation to differing contexts. For example, 'power to', although about an individual acting, can be them acting in a way that either promotes community cohesion or furthers sectarian conflict. Therefore, there must be recognition that power is practised over a range of levels and for a variety of reasons. Power can be utilised to strive for community cohesion and social change as much as it can be used to hinder or oppress people.

The powercube was based on the writings of Lukes (2004) and developed by Gaventa (2006) as a means for activists and practitioners to reflect on the 'possibilities of transformative action in various political spaces' (Gaventa, 2006, p. 25). The tool aids in exploration of the differing levels, spaces and forms of power, as well as the interrelationship between these. The powercube is used to analyse participation, action and decision-making within society. The interrelationships highlighted above, with the addition of 'power over' can also be analysed within the cube:

> "Power over" relations do exist and they warrant sustained critical attention—especially in the context of peace research, given that social justice is often an important precondition of peace.
>
> Karlberg (2005, p. 9)

Maintaining a multilevel analysis allows power to be assessed locally, nationally and globally. Of course, there can also be power analysis within each of these levels, such as power imbalances between localised communities, as will be discussed later. Spaces of power relate to the spaces where participation occurs and are divided between closed, invited and claimed spaces. Closed spaces can be macro-level spaces which are closed off to the majority of citizens, such as governmental international policies, but can also be closed spaces within small institutions, where citizens do not have access. Invited spaces are those which people are invited to participate in with set boundaries. Whilst claimed spaces are those which are often claimed by citizens on particular issues, these can be organic spaces (Cornwall, 2002), spaces based on particular issues or common pursuits.

The forms of power directly link to Lukes work (2004) and are visible, hidden and invisible. Hidden power is devised through the creation of barriers and the maintaining of the norm by those in power and privilege. Invisible power:

> ... involves the ways in which awareness of one's rights and interests are hidden through the adoption of dominating ideologies, values and forms of behaviour by relatively powerless groups themselves.
>
> Powercube (2015)

This maintains cultural hegemony (Gramsci, 1971) where consciousness of rights, capacity and oppression has not yet been realised due to the subtle and hidden aspects of invisible power.

Analysing power on a number of intersecting levels can ensure that as practitioners we are acutely aware of power, how it can be manipulated and controlled, or how it can shift and be reclaimed, depending on space, place and relationship. We do not conform to the notion that power is static but rather see it as fluid and as varying across contexts. As Miller et al (2006, p. 5) conclude:

In reality, power is dynamic, relational and multidimensional, changing according to context, circumstance and interest. Its expression and forms can range from domination and resistance to collaboration and transformation. This is good news for social justice promoters whose strategies depend upon new opportunities and openings in the practice and structures of power.

CYW practitioners who are critically conscious to changing community contexts, circumstances and interests can thus, seek to make power visible in order to work with communities and young people in developing new opportunities and openings for empowerment to be realised.

Empowerment

The multilevel analysis of power has an impact on the notion of empowerment; given that someone can have power in one context but not another. However, if power is viewed as relational, fluid and '… shapes the very conditions and possibilities for action' (Petit, 2012, p. 13); then the synergy between a power and empowerment is evident. Moreover, if power is resisted in its numerous sites and particularly through a process of 'self-transformation through the minimisation of states of domination' (Butin, 2001, p. 158) then the need for a process in working towards empowerment is clear.

The terminology of empowerment has shifted from its first conception where it had a strong political meaning, a focus on social change, equality, and social justice (Batliwala, 2007). Arguably, the fundamental problem in contemporary usage of the term empowerment is a failure to recognise, acknowledge and discuss the importance of power (Boje and Rosile, 2001; Hardy and Leiba-O'Sullivan, 1998). Further, the term can be assumed to mean that people can be empowered by benevolent others. The misappropriation of the terminology of empowerment by managerialist, neo-liberal agendas offering a tokenistic form of engagement, as opposed to the initial focus on social and political processes within a broader fight for social justice, is problematic. As Batliwala (2007, p. 563) argues:

> … in keeping with the insidious dominance neo-liberal ideology and its consumerist core, we see the transition of empowerment out of a realm of societal and systematic change and into individual domain—from a noun signifying shifts in social power to a verb signalling individual power, achievement, status.

Originally, empowerment is a process of working with people to support them to make positive decisions on their lives, in striving for a more socially just society. However, like any term with 'marketability', there is a danger that it can be co-opted into another sphere, with a different focus and lack of analysis. The analysis of organisational human relations (Boje and Rosile, 2001) is not the purpose of this chapter, nor are the debates entailed therein. However, unlike Batliwala (2007), we believe empowerment can still be useful, particularly when working within the youth and community field where emancipatory practice can be realised through a process of empowerment. Empowerment is to be critically conscious of the power dynamics prevalent within society and utilising this knowledge in ways that can positively shape and effect society, the 'capacity to make effective choices … and then transform those choices into desired actions and outcomes' (Alsop et al., 2006, p. 10). The empowerment process involves people making decisions and taking action that enables them to make real choices that are relevant to their contexts. The capacity for decision making and action relies on both agency and opportunity, where agency is linked to the ability to make choices, and opportunity is tied to the structural contexts in which the social actor, or social group, lives. However, empowerment should not be viewed as being solely relating to an individual (Ord, 2007) and can relate to groups of people and communities as will be discussed in more detail later. This opens a possibility to consider empowerment in the context of a fluid bricolage of communities.

Being a CYW practitioner is an educative role, which involves responsibility. In the process of facilitating capacity for decision making there should be open dialogue while adopting a 'critical friend' role (Gormally, 2012) in discussing 'problematic choices' (Ord, 2007), and the avoidance of exclusionary practices and harmful actions. As Jacques (1996) argues, the feeling of empowerment is not the same as being empowered. As such, empowerment should be a critical process, which is fundamentally fostered in an attempt to change society for the better.

The taken-for-granted aspects of power need to be challenged in order to achieve a process of empowerment which from a Foucauldian position means that the 'exercise of power only remains tolerable by hiding itself within the everyday, the mundane and the intimate' (Ball, 2013, p. 145). Thus, the disempowerment of citizens can be maintained despite feeling empowered. Through various institutions, such as formal schooling, 'the learner is made visible, but power is rendered invisible, and the learner sees only the tasks and the tests which they must undertake' (Ball, 2013, p. 48). As Ellsworth (1989, p. 298) highlighted when critiquing critical pedagogy:

… "empowerment," "student voice," "dialogue," and even the term "critical"—are repressive myths that perpetuate domination.

Drawing on practice, Ellsworth (1989) found these concepts to be ahistorical and de-politicised (Cho, 2013) and found that empowerment, 'treats the symptoms but leaves the disease unnamed and untouched' (p. 306) arguing that oppressive structures often go unchallenged. This highlights a reason why any work to support community empowerment necessitates a power analysis and it should not be regarded as a complete label to be gained but rather empowerment is a dynamic process. Moreover, while acknowledging that 'voice' and other such concepts are not unproblematic, ensuring an anti-oppressive approach to voice and identity and to have recognition of voice is crucial. Empowerment in this context is not just about an individual feeling better but rather we assert the Freirian notion (1996) that, through raising critical consciousness, coupled with a power analysis, empowerment or 'radical empowerment', can be 'the transformation of consciousness from an acceptance of oppression/reality to a belief that reality can be changed' (Cho, 2013, p. 80).

'Conscious of the Balance—Activism over Tokenism'

The following section explores how power analysis and 'radical' empowerment practices are utilised in shifting power balances in youth work, community development and research. Whilst much more could be discussed on each, the broader analysis is curtailed to advocating for promoting community and youth activism as opposed to tokenistic approaches to participation, empowerment and power analysis. By this we see activism as being critically conscious of power, of having the capacity to assess the imbalances and to practice in a manner that strives to be emancipatory, explicit and truthful. In contrast, we acknowledge that at times practice can be tokenistic in raising awareness of power dynamics but does little to assess how these can be changed and so can demonstrate power 'over' considerably more than power 'with'. It is our assertion that through effective and emancipatory practice we can challenge tokenism in pursuit of activism; both in supporting others and being self-reflexive (see Chapter 6).

Shifting the Balance of Power—Youth Work

Young people's experience of power is influenced by, for example, factors of lifestyle and economics. In responding to this, Davies (2005) proposals for the balances of power to be tipped towards young people suggests possibilities, through youth work, to challenge and change the dominant discourses where negative stereotyping has made the achievement of equality difficult (Devlin, 2006).

However, 'tipping the balance' does not mean that adults give up power in favour of young people or that young people take power from adults. Power is not a static object to give to one person or the other. This negative view of power, suggests that power is exercised when people, who are regarded as superior, take control over others. In contrast to this popularised negative view of power (Kalberg, 2005), viewing power positively is much more fluid, as control shifts from adult to young person and back again through their interactions with each other (Hill, Davies, Prout & Tisdall, 2004). Power can be exercised from top down, bottom up and horizontally:

> If power is seen positively ... power emerges as a variable rather than zero-sum game. This means that there need not be clear winners and losers fighting over a fixed amount of power but rather that power is diffused throughout society and is generated in such a way that the benefits and costs may be shared by many different actors. Thus what matters is not only who has power but how power operates.
>
> Hill et al. (2004, p. 89)

The relational approach to analysing power suggests that young people cannot be given power like a gift, rather it varies depending on relationship, situation and context. Therefore, young people may have access to power in one context but feel powerless within another. Thus, there is a need for young people to be aware of the power dynamics at play and the role of youth workers to facilitate the empowerment process. 'Power relations shift and are transformed ... [and where] ... a closer analysis of power relationships and their impact on practice, is a prerequisite of the work we undertake' (Batsleer, 2008, p. 9).

In this way, the empowerment process should challenge young people's tokenistic participation in decision making, such as being limited to minimal decisions e.g., choosing the colour of the walls and the furniture in the youth cafe. As Batsleer (2008, p. 149) asserts:

> Participation means more than simply 'taking part'. It refers to young people's rights to have a say in ways that make a difference in decisions that affect their lives.

Participation has got to be more that a nod in the right direction but should value young people as having the 'transformative capacity' (Giddens, 1987), the power, to transform their own and others' lives. In youth and community contexts it has been noted that participation has begun to replace the language of empowerment (Ord, 2007). However:

> Empowerment cannot be achieved without having participation as a precursor; and that the level of participation will determine the level, if at all, of eventual empowerment.
>
> Barry (1996 in Ord, 2007, p. 50)

Meaningful participation underpins emancipatory youth work, which is based on power sharing relationships where in the truest sense young people and youth workers should take action together, with each other, rather than acting on behalf of each other. Yet, the principle of power sharing is not always evident in youth work and there are contradictions, for example in assumptions that adults relate to young people in a particular way, variously classified as participants, members or users of services, and where practice has been suggested as a powerful form of regulation and control (Powney, Furlong, Carmel and Hall, 1997; Jeffs and Smith, 2010, de St Croix, 2010). In this kind of youth work, power may be used by adult youth workers to regulate or control the actions of young people who are regarded as being in a subordinate position. This assumption cautions that even when relationships are built on friendly and trusting approaches, youth workers should be conscious of the power dynamic within the setting. The importance of an underpinning and emancipatory value base thus becomes paramount to the development of youth work practice as a discrete educational methodology rather than risk reducing it to an informal 'approach' to working with young people.

Shifting the Balance of Power—Community Development

'The basis of community development's transformative potential lies in its analysis of power in relation to changing political times' (Ledwith, 2011, p. 177). Within community development practice, the analysis of power up and power down is important. We also assert the need to analyse horizontal power which can be evident across all aspects of CYW practice. As noted earlier, micro levels of power are important in establishing a movement for social change. By assessing these levels of power, whilst having consciousness of macro-levels of power, transformation can occur (Ledwith, 2011). Power analysis is important in community development practice where there is often a tendency to focus on the application of an approach rather than the theoretical perspectives and its distinct disciplinary value base (Wallace, 2008). In contrast, a community development approach promotes collective action to change existing social conditions and to 'challenge inequality, in seeking emancipation through education' (Wallace, 2008, p. 745). This is achieved through a theorised methodological process of empowerment via a critical power analysis.

Acknowledging the relational aspect of power across multiple levels contributes to the process of social change. Analysis within individual, internal, community, external and strategic spheres provides a framework for assessing and acting on power relations (Gormally, 2012).

Individual analysis of experiences of power can be a useful starting point within practice. Exploring the real and perceived individual power dimensions can facilitate reflexivity on the 'self' and the impact this has on relations with others. Finding a language (Petit, 2012), exploring 'stories of everyday life' (Ledwith, 2011, p. 177) and transforming the abstract into practice can provide a 'springboard' to critique the normalised power dynamics on a multitude of levels and the relational power apparent in differing contexts.

Examining internal relations within communities and community groups can facilitate critical analysis as to who are the powerful voices in the community or group, who dominates, controls or takes responsibility for the group development work and the internal mechanisms aligned to its smooth running. This analysis can help communities to discover how to raise their aspirations for empowerment in striving to become more representative and democratic. This provides a framework to assess what voices are not present within the group, what normalised assumptions have been created and what reasons are provided for why these voices are not recognised or apparent. This exploration of internal power dynamics ensures that self-reflexivity occurs and that tokenistic empowerment is assessed and challenged. Moreover, people who are routinely marginalised and subject to inequality driven exclusion can, on a micro-level, facilitate social change through this process of power analysis, which contributes to community activism due to increased capacity for self-evaluation.

Community relations are multifaceted in connection to power analysis. Practitioners can facilitate communities to explore and question who holds the power within the community, what type of power and in what manner is that power being used. For example, questioning the level of power the community group has in various contexts and with whom they are able to relate or work alongside is an important first step. Can the community group provide a positive facilitative power role (O'Brien & Moules, 2007) or does it exclude and isolate certain groups within the community? In areas of conflict it is necessary to question if there are groups with negative, controlling power that restricts the safety to challenge or critique.

External relations are those power dynamics prevalent between one community and another, or between one community of interest or another. However, an understanding of any negative or controlling power is required if external relations are to achieve mutually beneficial outcomes. Thus, in facilitating internal power dynamics, there should be a guided emphasis to ensure that groups don't play a 'blame game' against others as a form of what Freire (1996) would call horizontal violence. Rather, that they analyse their own positions, their own prejudices and their own perceptions in engaging with people and communities that are different to themselves or their self-identified communities. This process facilitates critical reflection on whether the process of 'othering' is being utilised negatively to create an exclusive identity, where a 'secure base' is created within a community by highlighting the difference of others. As Young (2007, p. 12) argues:

> ... insecurities in economic position and status, coupled with feelings of deprivation in both these spheres, engender widespread feelings of resentment both in those looking up the class structure and those peering down. Such insecurities can be experienced as a sense of vertigo and, outside of the charmed sphere of the contented minority, such uncertainties are tinged with anger and dislike.

Practically then, this step of analysis ensures that socially constructed borders (Giroux, 2014) are dismantled and positive community relations are promoted. Analysing this through a power analysis framework should contribute to community cohesion. The raising of critical consciousness on power imbalances may facilitate community action across communities in order to challenge structural issues and in redressing the 'balance of power' (Davies, 2005) in marginalised communities' favour.

The role of the gatekeeper is important in any engagement with communities and has a key role in helping or hindering external relations. A gatekeeper is a person who can literally hold the gates open to a community and can, as quickly, shut them. Such people may have a political standing, a normalised authority or a vested interest in maintaining people either engaged with, or ostracised from, working with the broader community. The gatekeeping role can be a restrictor to engagement and to the process of empowerment. Particularly in areas of weak community infrastructure individuals or groups can prevent information, resources or support from reaching an area (see Healey and O'Prey, 2008). However, they can also be a 'go-between' and the 'insider/outsider' to communities (Agada, 1999, p. 75) advocating for the needs of community members. In some sense then the gatekeeper can be the holder of positive or negative visible power, while it can also wield hidden power.

The gatekeeper can be seen as a power-holder. Spending time to get to know this person, or people, is an important lesson in becoming an effective practitioner. This interplay between practitioner and gatekeeper can be a slow and difficult process but can have an impact on the development of power relations that are productive or destructive in community contexts. To achieve social change, this process must be carefully navigated.

An additional level of analysis is strategic power, which is important in assessing community relationships with local authorities and institutions, elected officials and politicians, and with statutory and voluntary agencies. to ensure a strong and participative way of working. Only by applying a power analysis lens to these relations is it possible to fully understand the roles and responsibilities of others, including duty bearers, to ensure that realistic expectations of 'other' are developed. Assessing where power lies and in what circumstances it can facilitate action can assist in understanding what policies need to be challenged and how engagement needs to be improved.

Power analysis can probe various spheres of power, how it is used and in what manner. For practitioners, it allows depth of discussion not only theoretically on power, but on the uses and outplaying of it in the kinds of community outlined in our bricolage. Being aware of the multiple levels of power is imperative in practice. As Pettit (2012) asserts, practitioners need to create spaces for 'ideal speech situations' (Habermas, 1987) to '... critically and question the ideologies that reproduce social order', (Petit, 2012, pp. 22–23). In community development, through a clear analysis of power on multiple levels, and ensuring a range of voices have the power to be involved and heard; empowerment can develop.

Shifting the Balance of Power—Research

As we have previously discussed (Gormally and Coburn, 2014), a nexus can be established between youth work practice and research. The same may apply to the skills gained through community development practice. Although not the central focus of this book, it is worth mentioning that power and empowerment are crucial concepts when partaking in research as well as practice. Mertens (2005) notes that generally research focuses on people's experiences of inequality and their lack of power, or their incapacity to behave in particular ways or to achieve particular positions. However, she argued that a recent turn in thinking had shifted the research position to a more positive view that 'has led to reframing research questions to focus on strengths' (Mertens, 2005, p. 106). This shift in perspective is consistent with a shift from a deficits view of young people towards an assets view in generic youth work, instead of focusing on negative aspects of their lives. Mertens' perspective makes a case for examining people's perceptions and experiences of the research process in an inclusive and empowering manner. In ensuring that the views of marginalised groups are articulated and conveyed it is also important that the voices spoken are effectively listened to and not in a tokenistic way. Clough and Nutbrown (2002) suggest that 'Radical listening—as opposed to merely hearing—is the interpretative and critical means through which "voice" is noticed' (p. 67). These authors suggest that radically listening to participants allows 'faithful interpretation' (Clough & Nutbrown, 2002, p. 82) of what is being heard.

In research, power sits with the participant, who ultimately has the right to withhold information or withdraw from the study at any time. However, control can often be located with the youth worker or researcher, and so their role in facilitating an environment that enables or encourages power sharing becomes critical as part of a process that is complex, relational and situational. It does not mean that power or control is extended fully in one direction or another, rather, power is negotiated between young people and youth workers through dialogue and a problem posing approach to learning (Freire, 1996). Drawing on youth work values and practices, the inherent power imbalances that are present in all research relationships may also be reduced and as such, these values and practices create possibilities for shifting power relations and the development of new collaborative research practices (Gormally and Coburn, 2014).

Conclusion

When working within youth work, community development or carrying out research within these sites, tokenistic approaches to empowerment are often found. However, when developed by a critically aware, reflexive practitioner these methods of involvement can rather be utilised as sites of exploration and for the raising of critical consciousness (Freire, 1996). Tokenistic engagement practices should be critiqued and challenged, allowing space for meaningful practices which strive for relational processes of empowerment.

There are undoubtedly more macro level constraints that we operate under, such as limitations or regulations that are applied by funders, management committees and governmental policy, to name a few. The question then for practitioners is how we stay true to our emancipatory goals in striving for social change under these constraints. As with power there are multiple levels of empowerment, tokenism and activism are two central approaches we have analysed from practice. The tokenistic approach runs counter to an activist approach which is critically informed and demonstrates conscientisation of the reality of these constraints and how to facilitate the capacity to challenge such hegemonic narratives. Our next chapter discusses how critical consciousness might be achieved through reflexivity in order to develop practice for social transformation.

Bibliography

Agada, J. (1999). Inner-city gatekeepers: An exploratory survey of their information use environment. *Journal of the American Society for Information Science, Special Issue: Youth Issues in Information Science*, 50(1), 74–85.

Alsop, R., Bertelsen, M. and Holland, J. (2006). *Empowerment in Practice, from Analysis to Implementation*. Directions in Development. Washington, DC: World Bank

Baker, J., Lynch, K., Cantillion, S. and Walsh, J. (2004). *Equality: From Theory to Action*. Basingstoke: Palgrave Macmillan.

Ball, S. (2013). *Foucault, Power and Education*. Oxon: Routledge.

Batliwala, S. (2007). Taking the power out of empowerment—An experiential account. *Development in Practice*, 17(4–5), 557–565.

Batsleer, J. (2008). *Informal Learning in Youth Work*. London: Sage.

Boje, D. M. and Rosile, G. A. (2001). Where's the power in empowerment? Answers from Follett and Glegg. *The Journal of Applied Behavioural Science*, 37(1), 90–117.

Butin, D. (2001). If this is resistance I would hate to see domination: Retrieving Foucault's notion of resistance within educational research. *Educational Studies*, 32(2), 157–176.

Cho, S. (2013). *Critical Pedagogy and Social Change: Critical Analysis on the Language of Possibility*. Oxon: Routledge.

Clough, P. and Nutbrown, C. (2002). *A Student's Guide to Methodology*, London: Sage.

Community Foundation for Northern Ireland. (2012). Evaluation of the communities in Transition 2. Programme available at http://www.communityfoundationni.org/publications, accessed 7 July 2016.

Cornwall, A. (2002). *Making Spaces, Changing Places: Situating Participation in Development*. IDS Working Paper 170. Brighton: IDS.

Davies, B. (2005). Youth work: A manifesto for our times. *Journal of Youth and Policy*, 88, 1–23.

De St Croix, T. (2010). Youth work and the surveillance state. In J. Batsleer and B. Davies (Eds.), *What Is Youth Work?* (pp. 140–152). Exeter: Learning Matters.

Devlin, M. (2006). *Inequality and the Stereotyping of Young People*. Dublin: Equality Authority.

Ellsworth, E. (1989). Why doesn't this feel empowering? Working through the repressive myths of critical pedagogy. *Harvard Educational Review*, 59 (3): 297–324.

Fabion, J. (Ed.) (2002). *The Essential Works of Foucault, 1954–1984: Vol. 3. Power*. London: Penguin Books.

Foucault, M. (1972). *Power/Knowledge, Selected Interviews and Other Writings*. New York: Pantheon Books.

Foucault, M. (1975). *Discipline and Punish: The Birth of the Prison*. New York: Random House.

Foucault, M. (1980). 'Body/Power' and Truth and Power'. In C. Gordon (Ed.), *Michel Foucault: Power/Knowledge*: London: The Harvester Press.

Foucault, M. (1988). *The History of Sexuality*, Vol. 1: London: Penguin.

Freire, P. (1996). *Pedagogy of the Oppressed* (Ramos, M. B., Trans.) (2nd Ed.). London: Penguin.

Gaventa, J. (2006). Finding the spaces for change: A power analysis. *IDS Bulletin*, 37: 5.

Giddens, A. (1987). *The Nation-State and Violence*. Orlando: University of California Press.

Giroux, H. (2014). No bailouts for youth: Broken promises and dashed hopes. In A. Ibrahim and S Steinberg (Eds.), *Critical Youth Studies Reader* (pp. 97–103). New York: Peter Lang.

Gormally, S. (2012). A social justice approach to community development. *The Irish Journal of Community Work*, Issue 3.

Gormally, S. and Coburn, A. (2014). Finding nexus: Connecting youth work and research practices. *British Educational Research Journal*, 40(50), 869–885.

Gramsci, A. (1971). *Selections from the Prison Notebook*. Edited and translated by Hoare, Q. and Smith, G. N. London: Lawrence and Wishart.

Habermas, J. (1987). *Theory of Communicative Action, Volume Two: Liveworld and System: A Critique of Functionalist Reason (Book)*. Translated by McCarthy, T. A. Boston: Beacon Press.

Hardy, C. and Leiba-O'Sullivan, S. (1998). The power behind empowerment: Implications for research and practice. *Human Relations*, 51(4), 451–483.

Healey, K. and O'Prey, M. (Eds.) (2008). The communities in transition programme policy and practice lessons. *Communities in Transition: A Report from the Communities in Transition Programme of the Community Foundation for Northern Ireland*. The Community Foundation for Northern Ireland.

Hill, M., Davis, J., Prout, A. and Tisdall, K. (2004). Moving the participation agenda forward. *Children & Society*, 18(2), 77–96.

Hunjan, R. and Keophilavong, S. (2010). *Power and Making Change Happen*. Fife: Carnegie UK Trust.

Jacques, R. (1996). *Manufacturing the Employee: Management Knowledge from the 9th to 21st Centuries*. London: Sage.

Jeffs, T. and Smith, M. K. (Eds.) (2010). *Youth Work Practice*. Hampshire: Palgrave MacMillan.

Karlberg, M. (2005). The power of discourse and the discourse of power: Pursuing peace through discourse intervention. *International Journal of Peace Studies*, 10(1), 1–23.

Ledwith, M. (2011). *Community Development: A Critical Approach*. Bristol: Policy Press.

Lukes, S. (1974; 2004). *Power: A Radical View* (2nd Ed.). New York: Palgrave MacMillan.

Mertens, D. M. (2005). *Research and Evaluation in Education and Psychology: Integrating Diversity with Quantitative, Qualitative and Mixed Methods*. London: Sage.

Miller, V., VeneKlassen, L., Reilly, M. and Clark, C. (2006). *Making Change Happen: Power-Concepts for Revisioning Power for Justice, Equality and Peace*. Washington, DC: Just Associates.

Morriss, P. (2006). Steven Lukes on the concept of power. *Political Studies Review*, 4, 124–135.

O'Brien, N. and Moules, T. (2007). So Round the Spiral Again: A Reflective Participatory Research Project with Children and Young People. *Educational Action Research*. London: Routledge.

Ord, J. (2007). *Youth Work Practice—Creating an Authentic Curriculum in Work with Young People*. Dorset: Russell House Publishing.

Pettit, J. (2012). Getting to grips with power: Action learning for social change in the UK. *IDS Bulletin*, 43: 3.

Power cube. (2015). http://www.powercube.net/analyse-power/forms-of-power/invisible-power/, accessed on 7 December 2015.

Powney, J., Furlong, A., Cartmel, F. and Hall, S. (1997). *Youth Work with Vulnerable Young People: Scottish Research in Education Report, Interchange 49*. Glasgow: Glasgow University.

Sen, A. (1985). Well-being, agency and freedom: The Dewey lectures 1984. *Journal of Philosophy*, 82, 169–221. Retrieved 10 May 2016 from http://www.freelogy.org/w/images/d/dc/Sen85.pdf

Wallace, D. (2008). Community education and community learning and development (post devolution). In T. Bryce and W. Humes, *Scottish Education (3rd Ed.), Beyond Devolution*. Edinburgh: Edinburgh University Press.

Young, J. (2007). *The Vertigo of Late Modernity*. London: Sage.

· 6 ·

CRITICAL REFLEXIVITY

Introduction

This chapter asserts that working towards a more equitable society can be achieved by ensuring that practitioners are critically reflexive and engage in consciousness-raising as regular practice. Thompson and Pascal (2012) note the theory which underpins reflective practice is underdeveloped and often not integrated with practice. Therefore, this chapter unpacks the theoretical, epistemological and ontological differences and distinctions between reflection, being reflexive and adopting a critically reflexive stance. Discussion is developed around the impact of professional identity on the work of community practitioners by asserting that being reflexive ensures a depth of understanding of who we are, our social context and our positionality in relation to 'other professions'. It argues that unless practitioners understand the impact that the 'self' can have on their practice it is difficult to promote agency amongst people they work with, in seeking social transformation. Drawing on the work of Taylor (2010), we suggest that 'emancipatory reflexive praxis' will facilitate self-reflection, critical reflexivity and ensure that it has a theoretical underpinning that informs practice towards social change.

We have drawn on previous work (Gormally and Coburn, 2014) to articulate our basis of constructo-interpretivist epistemology in understanding the construction of knowledge and the interpretation of this through reflexive practice. The chapter analyses reflection and reflective practice, drawing on traditional educational theories (Dewey, 1933; Schön, 1983, 1987) to provide a foundational basis of understanding. Critical reflection and reflexivity are discussed followed by the identification of five key areas in the process of utilising reflexive praxis in professional practice: Positionality, Personal Bias, Organisational/Project-Level Analysis, Disciplinary Positionality and Bias and Macro Level Analysis offer five tangible areas of exploration for practitioners and academics alike.

Value Base—Epistemology

Reflection, reflexivity and critical reflexivity come from a particular value base which is usefully conceptualised by Thompson (2010) as 'theorising practice'. This is a fluid approach to practice which aims to integrate theory and practice (Thompson and Pascal, 2012). Taylor (2010) has devised a three-tier reflective model based on critical theory—technical, practical and emancipatory. This framework explores categories of knowledge and how these have an impact on the reflective process adopted. Technical reflection is influenced by scientific knowledge and is highlighted as being important to the healthcare professions, where Taylor's work is focussed. Technical reflection provides evidence and knowledge that is seen as rational and empirically sound. It does not provide scope for interpersonal connections or for power analysis:

> … and it will not provide a radical critique of the unexamined assumptions about social, economic, historical and cultural influences that underlie the instrumental action in procedural activist, because it does not have an interest in power and transformative action.
>
> Taylor (2010, p. 89)

The second type of knowledge explored by Taylor (2010) is practical reflection. This focuses on human interactions and allows an exploration of experiences and interpretation of context and subjectivity. This is a counter approach to the technical knowledge basis due to its subjective focus on human interactions. Although this can increase someone's awareness and can be useful to draw on in future engagements, it does not have transformative action at the heart of the process. The third sphere, emancipatory reflection, is also about human interactions but with the central focus on transformative action. At this level, there is a critiquing of power relations, of social roles and responsibilities in order to bring about change on social and political levels:

> Emancipatory reflection also offers you the potential to identify your own misguided and firmly held perceptions of yourself and your roles, to bring about positive change. The process of emancipatory reflection for change is praxis.
>
> Taylor (2010, p. 90)

Taylor (2010) is adamant that no type of knowledge and reflection supersedes another, instead arguing differing forms of knowledge have their place and can be useful in differing circumstances. Despite this, our focus here is that emancipatory knowledge aligns more with reflexivity than reflection. As a practitioner having gained technical and practical knowledge using reflection there should be a progression to emancipatory knowledge via reflexivity (Lipp, 2007).

Bleakley (1999) offers a detailed critique of the underpinning epistemologies of reflective practice. Fundamentally, this cautions that, 'reflection has become a by-word for introspective personalism, an internal act of thinking about thinking' (p. 320). Critiquing reflection as being grounded in technical-rational Enlightenment doctrine, Bleakley (1999) highlights that the ability for humans to think about thinking can be unreflexive and uncritical of the 'epistemological and ontological status of the "thinker"' (p. 325). The danger apparent here is that value-based assumptions become normalised without a critical element to reflexivity and result in a descriptive account that fails to problematize experience and interactions. Rather, holistic reflexivity 'is an inclusive ecological or caring act of reflection as well as an appreciative gesture, with an explicit concern for "otherness" and "difference"' (Bleakley, 1999, p. 328). Similar to Taylor (2010), Bleakley (1999) does not view holistic reflexivity as a pinnacle of the reflection process or as morally more defensible; instead it is a more complex, detailed, and demanding yet satisfying practice.

The concept of critical reflexivity is then an ontological endeavour which can be used in an empowering process of social transformation. Although for the kind of complex processes envisaged in CYW contexts, a stepping stone approach from reflection to reflexivity to critical reflexivity is too simplistic and rather we suggest practitioners need to use all in order to strive for a more just society.

As discussed previously (Gormally and Coburn, 2014), we advocate for a constructo-interpretive epistemology. The constructionist and constructivist approach to knowledge provides a foregrounding that reality is co-constructed by people both individually and as a part of groups. An interpretative stance also allows evaluation and reflection on people's experiences and realities. This approach must engage with a power analysis, as discussed in Chapter 5, to gain a theoretical understanding of the construction and interpretation of knowledge. However, heeding Bleakley's (1999) warning we are clear to avoid a reflective process where everything is an interpretation of another interpretation, or everything is an internal reflection of another reflection which has little transformative meaning or impact beyond reflecting for reflecting sake. To counter this relativist standpoint, we suggest that a constructo-interpretive epistemology usefully recognises that multiple views are sought (Gormally and Coburn, 2014). This can then be a foundational epistemology for 'emancipatory reflexive praxis' as a tool for practitioners who are engaged in empowering and emancipatory praxis.

Reflection and Reflective Practice

Reflection can be seen as drawing from educational philosophy (Dewey, 1933). In its simplest form, reflection is having the capacity to think about what has happened in a particular situation. It is to view things from various angles and to consider why (Bolton, 2014)? Dewey (1933, p. 6) defined reflection as:

> … active, persistent, and careful consideration of any belief or supposed form of knowledge in the light of the grounds that support it and the further conclusions to which it tends.

Utilising reflection as a practitioner, reflective practice, is to make sense of the world and to question those involved in each situation. Schön (1983; 1987) explained how as practitioners we work within the 'swampy lowlands' where we do not have the luxury or capacity to stand on a cliff and survey the land below. Instead we must use methods to learn our way through the lowlands; 'reflective practice makes maps' (Bolton, 2014, p. 3) so we can find a way and learn from experiences. Ghaye (2008) identifies five areas of reflection—values, feelings, thinking, actions and context to facilitate an understanding of experiences. Reflecting on all of these areas of practice helps create what Kolb (1983) has called a continual process of learning and relearning which ensures a more thorough understanding of how these experiences occur (Sapin, 2013). This process of continual reflection can have an impact on future practice and also become part of an educative process for practitioners and learners in transforming their knowledge and understanding of the world.

Schön (1987) differentiated between reflection-in-action and reflection-on-action. The former is calling on previous experiences and knowledge whilst in practice to help ensure that we use appropriate theories and values to support practice across a range of different and sometimes unexpected or unfamiliar learning environments. In this way, reflection-in-action draws on tried and tested knowledge or practice, and prevents working on ill thought out assumptions, which can have a detrimental impact on those we are working with. The latter, reflection-on-action, allows practitioners to reflect after the event has taken place. This allows them to reflect, for example, on how things went, what they might have done differently, and how this may have impacted on the event, which in turn should help them to improve their practice capabilities in future events when reflection-in-action is necessary.

Although reflection is undeniably beneficial for the individual practitioner and those they work with, it should impact much more:

> The route is through spirited enquiry leading to constructive developmental change and personal and professional integrity based on deep understandings.
>
> Bolton (2014, p. 11)

However, for Brookfield (1995, p. 8) 'Reflection is not, by definition, critical'. Therefore, to progress the reflective process, criticality with action, needs to be at the core. The next session discusses how the capacity to reflect becomes a critical pursuit which seeks to develop depth of understanding.

Critical Reflection

Critical reflection can be seen as questioning deeper level assumptions (Askeland and Fook, 2009) or as critical thinking and can be linked to critical theory (Holmes et al., 2005). Criticality on its own does not necessarily have to be reflective or reflexive but can be following critical principles (Askeland and Fook, 2009). Similarly, reflective practice does not have to be critical. Nevertheless, critical thinking is important to practitioners in order to facilitate a critique of power dynamics and practice relations. As Brookfield (2009) argues critical reflection is based on challenging assumptions and analysing power relations. Often such assumptions are reinforced through hegemonic ideologies (Gramsci, 1971). Thus, the ability to critically assess these ideological or common sense assumptions about practice allows a questioning of purpose, meaning and practices of both ourselves and others—including institutions and systems in society. For Humphrey (2009, p. 384) critical reflection is:

> ... the capacity to adopt an alternative standpoint from which a phenomenon can be critiqued in a coherent and communicable manner for the purpose of envisioning

constructive change. It involves going beyond the concrete facticities of everyday life so that they can be 'reframed' with reference to cultural contexts and conceptual schema.

This capacity to take a different view in order to re-frame practice means that criticality aligns with reflexivity, where instead of solely reflecting on the way things happen, critical refection and reflexivity seek to ask why they happen. Utilising a critical lens allows practitioners to question underlying assumptions, to question their impact, and where and why they have been perpetuated. By ensuring a level of criticality we can question and make visible our assumptions in regard to social phenomena, how these assumptions impact on our social relations and on the normative assumptions we perpetuate in our practice. This level of self-critical reflection underpins the process of reflexivity.

Reflexivity

Lynch (2000) has provided a reflexivity inventory including reflexivity in psychology and systems theory to more 'radical' conceptions. This chapter does not seek to replicate such extensive lists but rather discusses reflexivity as relational to community and youth workers. There has been much sociological debate surrounding the importance of reflexivity (Holmes, 2010). Bourdieu (1990) argued for reflexive sociology, where sociologists must be aware of their own positioning and their own internal structures but he also saw this as being applicable to the whole sociological field in assessing theories and assumptions of the social world which could be useful to CYW practitioners.

Reflexivity is often focused on the individual as a thinker (Bleakley, 1999), particularly when using reflection as a starting point for transformative learning. Giddens (1990) analyses reflexivity as a process about the changes people make within their lives due to their knowledge of their social context. However, Burkitt (2012) argues that this individualistic approach negates the construction of self-identity being formulated in relation to interactions and relations with others. In a similar individualistic positioning, Beck (1992) analyses reflection as knowledge and reflexivity as self-confrontation due to modernisation and individualisation. Beck (1992) makes a distinction between reflection and reflexivity, with reflexivity being reflection-free change in society due to modernisation. In contrast, Holmes (2010) contends that these cannot be dislocated as 'Social processes may have unintended consequences, but this does not mean that the reproduction of the social involves no reflection' (Holmes, 2010, p. 141). As Hibbert (2012, p. 805) notes:

If the patterns of our foundational assumptions change as a result of the process of reflexivity (and if they do not, the process is futile), then the actual process of thinking is also changed. Therefore, reflexivity is reflective, but it is also recursive.

Bourdieu and Wacquant (1992, p. 50) also critiqued the notion that this practice is narcissistic and argued that epistemic reflexivity is to '... destroy the myths that cloak the exercise of power and the perpetuation of domination'. Therefore, the practice in itself is useful to practitioners in order to raise critical consciousness and become critically aware of social relations through drawing on relevant theory and practice knowledge.

This similarly aligns with the previously proposed epistemological stance of constructo-interpretive (Gormally and Coburn, 2014) due to the necessity to understand individual and others' or multiple interpretations of the constructed social world. Instead of focussing solely on the individual, it is important to consider how being reflexive in regards to CYW as a social practice impacts on and changes social relations. Thus, it is necessary to move beyond individualised change within the social world and move towards putting critical reflexivity in action to change the social world in connection with others. Undoubtedly, in changing the social world and in connecting with others, emotions and awareness of the emotional relationship (Burkitt, 2012) is crucial. As connections and relations change then the process of thinking about these engagements will also have changed and therefore the reflexivity process should be reflected upon.

Lipp (2007) drawing on the knowledge types of Taylor (2006) views reflexivity as a deeper process than reflection. Tracking reflexive typologies, Lipp (2007) differentiates between Micro, Meso, and Macro levels of reflexivity. Micro is concerned about the individual, Meso is focussed on the organisational/project level, whilst macro is at the societal level. Lipp (2007) argues that being informed and 'enlightened' at a micro/individual level can facilitate differing perspectives on both a Meso and Macro level. This she argues, 'facilitates empowerment and emancipation as the practitioner gains insights into their situation reflexively' (Lipp, 2007, p. 24).

Reflexivity can also change the basis of societal interactions thus for Giddens (1990) trust is important due to the way modernity can produce uncertainties. However, this trust for Giddens is not in people but rather in abstract capacities (Holmes, 2010). In contrast, we would argue that for CYW practices trust and rapport, as discussed in Chapter 5, is important in building reflexive interactions both within oneself and with others. There must be trust in the process, trust in the uncertainty and trust in finding a new journey together which may be a difficult process, particularly given it may run counter to the normative hegemonic discussions which perpetuate oppositions between people within society.

However, as Lynch (2000, p. 36) highlights, '… what reflexivity does, what it threatens to expose, what it reveals and who it empowers depends upon who does it and how they go about it.' In addition, Lynch notes that trying to 'be' reflexive does not necessarily correlate with the outcome of that process. There are numerous unknowns in the process and the way in which some perceive the reflexive process may vary and so sometimes there is no unified outcome of critical consciousness raising or 'illumination' of the unknown. This leads us to question how, as practitioners, we can be reflexive whilst 'trusting in the processes and engaging with others?'

This chapter cannot set out a pre-prescribed set of instructions on how to be reflexive. As Lay and McGuire (2010, p. 543) note, reflexivity '… is not something that educators *do* to learners but it may be *facilitated* as collaborative process (emphasis in original).' However, as each person's learning process is unique and each relationship and circumstance varied, there are no set rules to follow in order to be an effective reflexive practitioner in facilitating this collaborative process with community or youth work participants. Nevertheless, a range of key areas that need to be taken into consideration in order to strive for emancipatory reflexive praxis. The remainder of this chapter identifies key areas that are important in fostering reflexivity in CYW.

The Professional Practice Process

This section identifies five key areas that we suggest are useful in facilitating reflexivity in CYW practice. The first area explores positionality, a personal awareness of the self and how this can impact on engagements with others. The second evaluates personal bias, promoting an understanding of our underpinning ethics values and bias and how this impacts on our decision-making processes. The third section explores organisational/project level values and bias. This analyses the meso level of the organisation or project in which we work. It advocates the need to be reflexive on the organisational context and to question the purpose, impact and beneficiaries of the policies pursued. The fourth section analyses the disciplinary positionality and bias that can often subsume our consciousness. This promotes the need to be aware of working with other disciplines, aware of our own ingrained hegemonic practices and to challenge practitioners to look outside of our own discipline and learn from others in seeking to achieve a more socially just society. The final section analyses macro level analysis which reiterates the points made in Chapter 1 about the need to be aware of, and act upon, the current neo-liberal agenda which further seeks to marginalise and criminalise the most disadvantaged in our societies.

Positionality

On a daily basis we, as humans, often reflect on day-to-day activities. We question why someone acted in a particular manner, or tell a friend of the behaviours of others. We often think about what has happened in a particular situation and can sometimes critique the social situation. We ask, albeit often unconsciously, questions such as—

- What happened?
- Why did it happen?
- What impact did that have on others?
- What could I have done differently?
- What could they have done differently?

These questions aid and support social interaction. They may help us to understand the world and to describe and explain a particular situation. However, positionality is much more than this and is about our role within a particular situation. Positionality is being aware of gender, race, educational achievements, economic position, etc. Questions such as, but not limited to, may include:

- How does my gender and others interpretation of this impact on this situation?
- How does my race and others interpretation of this impact on this situation?
- How does my educational status and others interpretation of this impact on this situation?
- How is my sexual orientation and others interpretation of this interpreted?
- How is my economic status and others interpretation of this viewed?

These questions allow us to think about how we are viewed by others and to understand how our position in society can have an impact on social relations. For the cynics, these might seem as if they are 'thinking for thinking's sake'. However, to understand yourself and to be critically aware of how others view you is important in analysing social relations but also to contribute to social change. If we are unaware of the perceptions we present or the assumptions people may make, then we can find ourselves isolating and ostracising those we are trying to engage. Moreover, not all of the interpretations may be assumptions. Sexual orientation, gender, age, sex, race, religion, economic status, educational achievements, etc. are all extremely important to the role you find yourself in or the time others may afford to you. Acknowledgement of positionality also allows us to be aware of those times or circumstances when we are afforded a position of power due to our perceived, or real, position within society. For example, you may gain a seat at the table or be turned away solely based on positionality. Being aware of this then allows negotiation, recognition and appreciation of the impact this plays but it does not need to prevent engagements with people of different positions rather it helps to acknowledge and address them in the reflexive process.

Personal Bias

Bias is a topic often discussed in relation to research. In previous work (Gormally and Coburn, 2014, p. 879) we argued:

> ... reflexivity can actively embrace and accommodate bias throughout the whole research process and being reflexive on personal, implicit values does not necessarily require that these are sidelined or bracketed. Rather an acknowledgment of such values and their impact upon the research will enrich the research process and enhance analytical argument.

This process of reflecting on bias is also useful in practice. The reflection process is not used in order to 'bracket off' the bias as some phenomenologist researchers (Husserl, 1989; Ahern, 1999) would argue. It is not to pretend they do not exist in social interactions but rather, to be reflexive, is to be aware of your own values, where they came from and the impact these have on others. The bias we hold may be so normalised it is difficult to acknowledge or to comprehend as being a bias at all. Being brought up in a certain culture, with cultural norms that have an impact on how we view ourselves and others. Similarly, societal norms and political discourses may become accepted and normalised in our everyday assumptions and be translated into ingrained bias and values which we do not critique or challenge. The role of women and men, the age at which people can vote, the sexual orientation of those who have or do not have children, the list could be endless.

As noted earlier, one of the criticisms of reflexivity is a narcissistic, individualistic bias that sometimes aligns with related literature. We advocate for an individual understanding leading to a social understanding. This means being reflexive on the impact of your views on social relations as well as on the perspectives of others. To be reflexive is to be able to view interactions and the construction of knowledge from differing angles. Thus, being aware of personal bias can assist an analysis of where others' bias may be evident. It can be a two-way process which can support and facilitate consciousness raising. This 'going beyond' personal reflection is highlighted by Lay and McGuire (2010, p. 542) who argue:

> Reflection may be an anecdote for the unexamined experience, but not without a structure that challenges learners to stretch beyond their personal beliefs and values in consideration of alternative knowledge.

As Maxey (1999, p. 201) notes in a study on activism:

> By actively and critically reflecting on the world and our place in it, we are more able to act in creative, constructive ways that challenge oppressive power relations rather than reinforce them.

Working with others to be aware of their own normalised bias or the impact their values, ethics, and bias have on their treatment of others will help to build understanding, cohesion and positive social action.

Organisational/Project Level Analysis

The critical analysis of positionality and personal bias begins with focussing on individual interactions, albeit within a social context. The next layer of complexity for practitioners to be reflexive on is the meso level (Lipp, 2007), the organisational/project level. This encourages people to be reflexive on the organisational context in which they work, to critique and challenge the underpinning values and to assess the purpose of these and who they benefit. When working within an organisational context specific practices, values and bias may become normalised. The dominant voices apparent within the organisation may be uncritically accepted and the status quo of the day-to-day workings may be second nature to the practitioners. However, this level of reflexivity should begin to facilitate questions around—

- Who is the 'primary client?' (Sercombe, 2010)
- How have policies been introduced within the organisation?
- Who holds the power in decision making?
- What voices are missing from the negotiation processes?
- Who controls our funding streams and what impact does this have on our role in social transformation?
- Do we as practitioners socialise young people into existing dominant power structures without any critical reflection on the benefits/ negatives of these structures on young people? (Cooper, 2012)

To be critically reflexive at organisational or project level allows the formulation of action and strategic planning on how to engage with others. It facilitates a comprehension of the broader aims of our work and ensures that our critical reflexivity is informed by theory and practice that strives for emancipatory outcomes for those we work with. It also allows the constant challenging of processes and practices which may have become normalised. For example, an organisation may have jeopardised its core values and ethics in the pursuit of finances and sustainability but in doing so has failed to analyse the macro structural impact of policies which further structural disadvantage, discrimination and inequality, as will be discussed later. This practice ensures a refocussing on process, participation and collective rights by questioning who we are working for and if we are actually achieving our core aims.

Disciplinary Positionality and Bias

In addition to the organisational/project level analysis there is a broader reflexive process which needs to take place on our disciplinary bias. Within the fields of youth work, community development and adult education we may be able to see areas of commonality. This commonality is undoubtedly a strength and encourages us to articulate our underpinning ethics, values and goals for practice. However, we can also become so immersed in our fields of practice that we assume that others should have the same value set or goals. Moreover, we potentially become subsumed in our own narrative that we overlook other fields of practice which may provide boundary crossing opportunities (Coburn, 2010). Unlike Hibbert (2012, p. 817) we are not advocating that 'the desired attitude of reflexive enquiry should lead to a loosening of commitment to all particular ideological worldviews'. Rather, awareness of our worldview and a recognition of others' interpretation and disciplinary grounding, may open doors for our practice to develop in new and innovative ways whilst still staying true to our emancipatory purpose.

As the political context shifts, particularly within the United Kingdom, there are fewer practitioners being employed with 'youth work' or 'community development' within their job title. This does not mean that we forget about our practice nor ignore our emancipatory aims but it does means that we have to become acutely aware of our working context and create ways and means to work with others to develop a synthesised practice that critiques the structures in which we work. It means being open and transparent about our own aims whilst drawing on other professional practices which may support our aims and goals. Making sense of the world and creating new meanings by deconstructing borders takes us outside of current discourse to create new ideas or alternative forms of knowledge (Giroux, 2005). Being critically reflexive on our disciplinary positionality allows us to forge new networks, connections and communities of practice which can cross disciplinary boundaries in a manner which is beneficial to those we work alongside (see Chapter 9). It also allows us to develop a national and international scope to CYW practice and ensures we articulate this practice in a manner that is coherent and transferable to others within society.

Macro Level Analysis

To avoid self-introspection which 'focuses attention at the micro level as if social problems were the fault of a bad social agent rather than oppressive social policies and institutional practices' (Lay and McGuire, 2010, p. 546) we promote the need for a macro level analysis. As stated in Chapter 1 the current neo-liberal agenda has moved towards supporting practice that is focussed on punitive policies that individualises communities and young people. The 'criminalisation of social policy' (Rodger, 2008) which has been evident within contemporary political agendas can subvert our practice without gaining critical consciousness of the structural levels in which we operate. As Ball (2013, p. 130) notes:

> The move from the welfare state to the neo-liberal state involves a redistribution of responsibilities and the emergence of new forms of government—self-government.

This self-government and responsibility for survival results in more people being left in precarious positions and where young people are routinely viewed as the bottom of the power scale (Hamilton and Seymour, 2006). These rules and definitions need to be reflected and acted upon. We need to question if as practitioners we are adopting a narrative which relegates the most vulnerable in society to the position of 'denizens':

> A denizen is someone who, for one reason or another, has a more limited range of rights than citizens do.
>
> Standing (2011, p. 14)

We need to be clear that we do not subscribe to a deficit discourse that is utilised towards specific communities and groups of young people which results in practical intervention strategies which seek to 'fix' some element of these groupings deemed as not yet, if ever, full citizens. This deficit discourse can permeate all aspect of society and our disciplinary fields are not exempt. To ensure that we do not subscribe to this mantra we need to rearticulate our practice in emancipatory terms and to strive for radical social change (Baker et al., 2005) through macro level analysis and by translating this critical consciousness into action (Standing, 2011).

Conclusion

This chapter has sought to provide an overview of reflection, critical reflection and reflexivity. It accepts that one approach is not the pinnacle (Bleakley, 1999; Taylor, 2010) of becoming a fully rounded practitioner and a stepping stone approach through a linear process is not necessarily viable. Rather the chapter provides an overview of theoretical viewpoints on highly contested concepts and articulates areas of exploration that would be useful to practitioners. We assert, as in Chapter 5, that there is a need for a power analysis to be included in reflexive practice. We draw on Taylor (2010) who articulates that emancipatory reflection has a central focus on transformative action. For Taylor (2010), the way to achieve emancipatory reflection is through the process of praxis. We have drawn on this formulation and from our discussion in Chapter 3, we argue that youth and community work practitioners should adopt emancipatory reflexive praxis ensuring the inclusion of criticality, the analysis of power dynamics and awareness of theory and practice knowledge that underpins our emancipatory process. We have identified five key areas where emancipatory reflexive praxis can take place and have shown how this can be used as a means to explore micro, meso and macro

(Lipp, 2007) aspects of our practice. This list is not exhaustive and as discussed in the next chapter, there are numerous practicalities of making this process happen. Nevertheless, we believe that emancipatory reflexive praxis can raise consciousness personally and can also be used as a tool for CYW practitioners to facilitate consciousness rising in communities to ensure that positive social change and social transformation can be achieved, for the benefit of all, not only the powerful few.

Bibliography

Ahern, K. J. (1999). Ten tips for reflexive bracketing. *Qualitative Health Research*, 9(3), 407–411.

Askeland, G. A. and Fook, J. (2009). Critical reflection in social work. Editorial. *European Journal of Social Work*, 12(3), 287–292.

Baker, J., Lynch, K., Cantillion, S. and Walsh, J. (2004). *Equality: From Theory to Action*. Basingstoke: Palgrave Macmillan.

Ball, S. (2013). *Foucault, Power and Education*. Oxon: Routledge.

Beck, U. (1992). *Risk Society*. London: SAGE Publications.

Bleakley, A. (1999). From reflective practice to holistic reflexivity. *Studies in Higher Education*, 24(3), 315–330.

Bolton, G. (2014). *Reflective Practice: Writing and Professional Development*. London: SAGE Publications.

Bourdieu, P. (1990). *The Logic of Practice*. Cambridge: Polity Press.

Bourdieu, P. and Waquant, L. (1992). *An Invitation to Reflexive Sociology*. Chicago: University of Chicago Press.

Brookfield, S. D. (1995). *Becoming a Critically Reflective Teacher*. San Francisco: Jossey-Bass.

Brookfield, S. D. (2009). Engaging critical reflection in corporate America. In Mezirow, J and Taylor, E. (Eds).*Transformative Learning in Practice: Insights from Community, Workplace and Higher Education* (pp. 125–136). San Francisco: Jossey Bass.

Burkitt, I. (2012). Emotional reflexivity: Feeling, emotion and imagination in reflexive dialogues. *Sociology*, 46(3), 458–472.

Coburn, A. (2010). Youth work as border pedagogy. In J. Batsleer and B. Davies (Eds.), *What Is Youth Work?* Exeter: Learning Matters.

Cooper, C. (2012). Imagining "radical" youth work possibilities—Challenging the "symbolic violence" within the mainstream tradition in contemporary state-led youth work practice in England. *Journal of Youth Studies*, 15(1), 53–71.

Dewey, J. (1933). *How We Think: A Restatement of the Relation of Reflective Thinking to the Educative Process*. Boston: D.C. Health.

Ghaye, T. (2008). *Building the Reflective Healthcare Organisation*. Oxford: Blackwell.

Giddens, A. (1990). *The Consequences of Modernity*. Palo Alto: Stanford University Press.

Giroux, H. A. (2005). *Border Crossings: Cultural Workers and the Politics of Education*, 2nd Edition. New York: Routledge.

Gormally, S. and Coburn, A. (2014). Finding nexus: Connecting youth work and research practices. *British Educational Research Journal*, 40(50), 869–885.

Gramsci, A. (1971). *Selections from the Prison Notebooks of Antonio Gramsci*. International Publishers: New York.

Hamilton, C. and Seymour, M. (2006). ASBOs and behaviour orders: Institutionalized intolerance of youth? *Youth Studies Ireland*, 1(1), 61–76.

Hibbert, P. (2012). Approaching reflexivity through reflection: Issues for critical management education. *Journal of Management Education*, 37(6), 803–827.

Holmes, M. (2010). The emotionalization of reflexivity. *Sociology*, 44(1), 139–154.

Holmes, P., Cockburn-Wooten, C., Motion, J., Zorn, T. and Roper, J. (2005). Critical reflexive practice in teaching management communication. *Business Communication Quarterly*, 68, 247–256.

Humphrey, C. (2009). By the light of the Tao. *European Journal of Social Work*, 12(3), 377–390.

Husserl, E. (1989). *Ideas Pertaining to a Pure Phenomenology and to a Phenomenological Philosophy*. Norwell: Kluwer Academic Publishers.

Kolb, D. (1983). *Experiential Learning: Experience as the Source of Learning and Development*. New York: Prentice Hall.

Lay, K. and McGuire, L. (2010). Building a lens for critical reflection and reflexivity in social work education. *Social Work Education: The International Journal*, 29(5), 539–550.

Lipp, A. (2007). Developing the reflexive dimension of reflection: A framework for debate. *International Journal of Multiple Research Approaches*, 1(1), 18–26.

Lynch, M. (2000). Against reflexivity as an academic virtue and source of privileged knowledge. *Theory, Culture & Society*, 17(3), 26–54.

Maxey, I. (1999). Beyond boundaries? Activism, academia, reflexivity and research. *Area*, 31(3), 199–208.

Rodger, J. J. (2008). *Criminalising Social Policy: Anti-Social Behaviour and Welfare in a De-Civilised Society*. Cullompton: Willan.

Sapin, K. (2013). *Essential Skills for Youth Work Practice* (2nd Ed.). London: SAGE Publications.

Sercombe, H. (2010). *Youth Work Ethics*. London: Sage.

Schön, D. (1983). *The Reflective Practitioner*. New York: Basic Books.

Schön, D. (1987). *Educating the Reflective Practitioner*. San Francisco: Jossey-Bass.

Standing, G. (2011). *The Precariat: The New Dangerous Class*. London: Bloomsbury Academic.

Taylor, B. (2006). *Reflective Practice: A Guide for Nurses and Midwives*. Buckingham: Open University Press.

Taylor, B. (2010). *Reflective Practice for Healthcare Professionals*. Maidenhead: Open University Press.

Thompson, N. (2010). *Theorizing Social Work Practice*. London: Palgrave Macmillan.

Thompson, N. and Pascal, J. (2012). Developing critically reflective practice. *Reflective Practice: International and Multidisciplinary Perspectives*, 13(2), 311–325.

· 7 ·

AN ALTERNATIVE SOCIAL VISION

This chapter analyses questions about who we work for and why we do this kind of work. It challenges practitioners to reflect on who the real beneficiaries of their work are and whether youth and community work can be tokenistic, or uses core concepts but does not deliver in practice, thus becoming complicit with political ideologies that counteract a social model for equality and social justice. The chapter questions the kind of practices that aspire towards the creation of a more equitable and socially just society, and challenges whether practitioners are identifying and addressing structural disadvantage, discrimination and inequality by refocusing on process, participation and collective rights.

As noted within the previous chapter we have advocated the need to explore macro level agendas and question the normative societal structures in which we operate. This chapter therefore seeks to articulate an overview of the current context in which our practice is situated. We are aware that internationally there are variations on this context and that we cannot provide an individualised summary of these differences. As such we begin from the starting point that our work is generally taking place under a patriarchal, neoliberal, capitalist agenda which seeks to dominate, individualise and marketise. This chapter sets this context but then offers a vision for an alternative social vision. It assesses how this vision might be achieved and challenges whether, as practitioners, we are critically conscious in actively striving towards a more equitable society.

Current Context

As explored in Chapters 1 and 6, we have asserted a need to be critically aware of the context in which we CYW practice is developed. As community educators we have become accustomed to hearing students articulate their drive in 'wanting to make a difference' but then initially, uncritically subscribing to normative assumptions about sections of our communities and society. It is this context and these normative assumptions which must be challenged throughout our practice.

A capitalist system undeniably places a market value on people's capacity to sell labour (Marx and Engels, 1888, 2004). However, neo-liberalism has extended the marketability of everyone and everything to the point that a full range of everyday aspects or artefacts of life can be reduced to an economic value. The austerity agenda provided clear evidence of this doctrine, where the most vulnerable in society are now experiencing the brunt of neoliberal globalisation which seeks to intensify levels of poverty and human suffering (Bello, 2002). As articulated elsewhere (Hughes et al., 2014) show how the impact of this neoliberal policy reform has had a profound impact on wellbeing and people's capacity to provide effective service provision. Abramovitz and Zelnick (2010) explored social policy reform in the United States and South Africa and found that cutbacks had a direct and profound impact on 'caring' and on the capacity of service providers to provide services due to a reduction in staff time spent in each location and in the resources required to offer appropriate levels of support. Moreover, 'Welfare organising becomes increasingly marketised, and profit making overrides notions of social justice and caring' (Cooper et al., 2015, p. 6), which is increasingly concerning in light of extended life expectancy and the kind of services that may be needed, beyond a simple caring function, towards improving quality of life and the emergence of new social contexts for older people.

The marketisation of welfare and the focus on profit making has resulted in a deficit discourse that places blame on the individual and moves the gaze from structural inequalities perpetuated by structural dysfunction (Giroux, 2013) to 'fixing' people who are lacking the capacity to fit into this structure

(Hughes et al., 2014; Cooper et al., 2015). This has undeniably had an impact on the central focus of CYW practice:

> Over the past three decades, much youth work practice has been redirected at focusing on the perceived cultural 'deficits' of working-class and minority ethnic young people —with a subsequent emphasis on 'fixing' *their* 'problems'.
>
> Cooper et al. (2015, p. 9)

This individualisation of perceived non-conformity and being in deficit fails to consider the broader social context that places groups of people within a precariat (Standing, 2011). The precariat are somewhat different to an underclass (Murray, 1996) doctrine as the neo-liberal state want and need the precariat (Standing, 2011). However, as a result of increased educational expectations, reduced monetary worth and precarious positions within society, the precariat often experience the four As—anomie, alienation, anxiety and anger. The reality of being excluded from civil, cultural, social, economic and/ or political rights which are associated with full citizenship and thus occupying the role of 'denizens' (Standing, 2011; 2014) results in a policy context which simultaneously needs, yet also excludes, many within society. This particularly resonates with people who are excluded from political process making it difficult to assert their rights as citizens due to for example, age, ability or race (Bessant, 2007; de St. Croix, 2010; Taylor, 2010).

This policy context results in young people being seen as dangerous or invisible (Giroux, 2014). Moreover, this problematizing of behaviours can result in those working with young people to undermine their emancipatory values and either unconsciously or instrumentally adopt:

> … ways of working which are in contrast to their values, guiding young people to be entrepreneurial in making a 'self' that is acceptable and conforms to a normative ideal; a fiscally-active citizen of the future, desired, and 'nudged' by the government and youth work interventions.
>
> Hughes et al., (2014, p. 7)

Of course these neo-liberal policy interventions are not focussed on all young people or on all communities. Rather, as Clarke notes, the dominant representations of 'problem' youth sees them described as marginal, criminal or 'youth of migrant origin' (Clarke, 2009, p. 310). The communities targeted by social welfare reform are often the most excluded and vulnerable with a focus on getting people back into employment, reducing the cost of social welfare and minimising the amount of state support available. In 2010, in the United

Kingdom the Coalition Government, made up of the Conservative Party and Liberal Democrats, 'placed conditionality and responsibility at the heart of welfare policy' (Beatty et al., 2015, p. IV). This places responsibility back on the individual and targets those who are not already engaged in the market system as being ineffective. As Young notes:

> Poverty is a stigma, because all of the institutions of society say so. The market flaunts its goods but denies you access to all but the most tawdry. It coerces you into work at the very lowest level it can, informing you in very clear monetary terms what you are worth: very little. It is an educational system which brands you as illiterate, a failure; a police force and criminal justice system which treats you blatantly with disrespect and disdain, and a welfare state which, with all its job schemes and back to work agencies, finally individualises you as a shirker, a loser. This is where self-blame and social stigma come together.
>
> Young (2007, pp. 76–77)

This self-blame and social stigma has an impact on the wellbeing of these targeted groups (Cooper, 2010). The necessity to take responsibility for personal wellbeing (Ball, 2013) and to deal with the precarious contexts in which community members are struggling to make a good life is a difficult balance to achieve in terms of challenge and/or survival. However, in order to achieve social change with the emancipatory values of social justice and equality the job of the CYW practitioner is precisely one of striking this balance.

An Alternative Vision

Our vision for the future is one where practitioners are acutely aware of the hegemonic norms which pervade our society. It is a future where critical consciousness is clearly articulated and where this becomes a cornerstone of our practice. We envisage a world, which may be criticised as being utopian, where practitioners work with others to identify the dominant discourses, to challenge the hegemonic norms and to unearth the negative political ideologies which seek to maintain people in positions of oppression. The vision we have for the future is one of awareness and of action. It is a vision that acknowledges injustice but then works with those who face the brunt of injustices in order to challenge them and to hold those perpetuating them to account. It is a society that is built on foundations of justice and equality. However, we are also realists. We acknowledge the difficulties practitioners face on a day-to-day basis and we know that practices with a social democratic underpinning are being eroded through the marketization of both ourselves as individuals and of our practice. Nevertheless, the remainder of this chapter asserts that we can work in small ways, achieving and striving for small wins which can help build momentum and confidence in making lasting social change. We do not assume that this practice is easy particularly given that:

> Critical ideas and concepts in support of a equality, justice, freedom and democracy, in particular, have lost their material and political grounding and have become sound bites either scorned by mainstream politicians or appropriated only to be turned into their opposite.
>
> Giroux (2016, p. 26)

Moreover, CYW practitioners are faced with:

> Class-based judgements on what is normative underpin the criteria by which the targets are measured and formulate a certain view of what young people should 'be' and what youth workers should 'do'.
>
> Hughes et al. (2014, p. 6)

The focus on reaching targeted outcomes may skew the notion of 'what works' and result in relatively meaningless outcomes being measured that provide only an impression of the value of youth work (Ord, 2007) as opposed to the reality of its value. The next section of this chapter therefore seeks to support our alternative vision by challenging hegemony and political ideologies, and articulating 'the society we want' (Knight, 2015). It questions why we do this work, rejecting the deficits based pathologising that is apparent in contemporary social contexts and addressing the question: who are the real beneficiaries of our practice?

Challenging Hegemony and Political Ideologies

The first task in articulating an alternative vision or 'reimagining' a different future is to be critically conscious of the neo-liberal hegemonic norms. Practitioners and the communities and groups they work with, need to be aware of the political ideologies that counteract a social model for equality and social justice. These hegemonic norms and political ideologies adopt a pathologising discourse, with 'quick fix' policy solutions and make a distinction between the 'deserving' and 'undeserving' poor. Critical comprehension helps people to understand what is Machiavellian about hegemonic norms, in that we not only subscribe to these norms but they are maintained despite their strengthening of the positions of those in power. The embeddedness of hegemonic norms in social systems, and in knowledge, ideas and discourse, make an alternative vision seem futile. Nevertheless, obtaining and retaining consciousness can ensure that critical theory is utilised to challenge a dominant ideological stance. As Brookfield notes in relation to adult education:

> From the perspective of critical theory, a critical adult is one who can discern how the ethic of capitalism, and the logic of bureaucratic rationality, push people into ways of living that perpetuate economic, racial and gender oppression. Additionally, and crucially, critical theory views a critical adult as one who takes action to create more democratic, collectivist economic and social forms.
>
> Brookfield (2005, p. ix)

Hegemony is pervasive in all societies (Gramsci, 1971) and is maintained through consent. However, it is our assertion that hegemonic norms do not need to be viewed as solely negative and contributing to the neo-liberal doctrine. Rather, in a reimagined future, hegemonic influences might perpetuate a norm that challenges oppression, discrimination and inequality by refocusing on process, participation and collective rights.

Throughout this book, we have continuously noted the need to raise critical consciousness, but this raises a question about how we do this? Again there is not one simple solution. Analysing consciousness in relation to specific institutions within society is challenging enough but to analyse the engrained nature of hegemony is difficult and at times, tiring. In attempting to articulate this process to a student recently they asked "But won't I just be paranoid about everything?" Despite not answering clearly at the time, a more appropriate response could have been—this is not paranoia, it is critical awareness, it is this consciousness of your surroundings that helps you to see the world differently. For Gramsci (1971, p. 333) standing 'apart' and being 'different' from culture may be an initial first step towards viewing the world differently. The second phase of this critically conscious learning is to evaluate the personal self within context, something discussed in Chapter 6. We advocate for emancipatory critically reflexive praxis as a means of becoming aware of personal positionality in addition to evaluating the political systems and contexts in which we are situated.

By being aware of both the underpinning political basis of perpetuated ideologies and the cultural hegemonic norms, we can ensure that we do not subconsciously or deliberately become complicit with a discourse that counteracts a social change model for equality and social justice.

The Society We Want—Why Do We Do This Work?

When awareness of the dominant neo-liberal hegemonic norms is realised, there is increased recognition of the requirement to articulate and commit to a collective vision for the future. Undoubtedly sceptics will suggest that this will never happen and that the market economy is so deeply ingrained on a global scale that any vision for the future which is based on emancipatory social change is unlikely, particularly given that neo-liberal values seem to 'permeate everything about life on earth' (Ledwith, 2011, p. 1). However, this is where we need to adopt a 'redressable goal' approach and begin with the capacity to articulate our main purpose of youth and community work as taking action for social change. As discussed previously (see Chapter 3), addressing redressable injustices (Sen, 2009) allows practitioners to engage in relatively 'easy wins' to build confidence, momentum and activist techniques in order to address broader social injustices and areas of inequality. To engage in this process, we need to be clear on why we do this work.

In a recent report carried out for the Webb Memorial Trust entitled 'The Society We Want' Knight (2015) found that from a survey of 10,112 people over the age of sixteen, 60.9 % of people felt 'A fair society' best described what they wanted from the notion of good society. Yet, as Knight notes:

> ... fairness means different things for different groups. For people who take a structural view of society, fairness is linked to equality where all individuals are treated equally regardless of class, ethnicity or contribution to society. For people who take an individualistic view of society, fairness is about contributing to society and only taking out what you've put in. Help to those in need is often seen to be conditional upon their contribution to society.
>
> Knight (2015, p. 26)

This suggests that the articulation of equality and fairness could and should be something that practitioners explore in more detail. We need to work with others to adopt a structural view on society, to be clear of the division between the wealthy and poor and to critique and challenge the patriarchal norms that permeate our societal structures and institutions.

The report drew on 12,000 individual views through a YouGov poll and twelve supplementary focus groups all based within the United Kingdom. Interestingly the report also found that there was no correlation between the priority of qualities that people wanted from a good society and what was already present within UK society. Almost everyone articulated that they want to remove absolute poverty but opinions were divided in relation to relative poverty. Only 8.5 % of people felt that the government should support unemployed people to have a basic income that is set at half of the average household income. Yet, 32.6 % felt that the government should provide enough money to avoid starvation and homelessness but nothing more. Despite the controversies in relation to welfare and governmental support, everyone involved in the study articulated that they 'want to live secure lives with good relationships and [that] this has a much higher priority than making lots of money' (Knight, 2015, p. 30).

This report, although UK specific, provides an insight into the type of society that people want. Despite debates about welfare payments and governmental support to the most vulnerable in society, there was an overwhelming desire for people to live in a society where absolute poverty is eradicated and fairness, security and good relationships are of utmost importance. This offers a small but crucial starting point in challenging the individual doctrine that suggests that people are solely 'out for themselves' and that gaining as much money as possible is the main driver for people within society.

This affirms a role for youth an community workers to challenge individualistic conceptions of society and to promote and develop a discourse of socially just emancipatory praxis through critical practice. It affirms the capacity to articulate for ourselves what type of society we want and the possibility to then work with others to do the same. We need to question why we do this kind work and if it is a part of a longer term, more radical vision for creating a better society. We are clear in our aims to strive for a more socially just society, one that challenges injustice and inequality and we feel that youth and community work offers one way of making a contribution. Elsewhere, Cooper et al., (2015) have rearticulated a similar reimagining aim with specific relation to young people, the education system and in challenging the 'lacking discourse'. Practitioners then need to be challenged, both by themselves, by educational institutions, colleagues and those they work alongside to articulate the kind of society they want and the reasons why they take forward particular practice. Once we have a clear conception of this vision we then need to work together with communities to find strategies that can facilitate ways and means in striving for that vision.

Rejecting Deficit Pathologising

Rejection of a pathologising discourse requires practice to promote critical awareness of the pathologising rhetoric which often seeps into the broader neo-liberal policy discourse. As a deficits discourse implies that people in society are lacking some crucial aspect to their being which makes it difficult for them to feel part of, or to fit within, the dominant social structures and contexts as 'blame' is placed on the individual, not the structure. As mentioned earlier, this rhetoric is clear when analysing the labelling of young people or communities in deprivation. Drawing on the phraseology of 'gang talk' (Hallsworth and Young, 2008), we articulate our concern about a kind of 'youth talk' which pathologises young people and blames them for not conforming to expectations pre-set by others.

In practice, this means that we have to critically challenge this discourse and moreover should not subscribe to superficial programmes of work which actually seek to further exclude, marginalise or isolate those with whom we work. We must consciously act, in order to challenge such programmes which are specifically in place to change behaviour that socialises young people into pre-existing dominant structures of power (Cooper, 2012). We need to question the targeted interventionist, crime prevention agenda (Wallace and Coburn, 2003) that is often associated with practice that routinely categorises and criminalises young people as deviant (Barber, 2007; Morgan and O'Hare, 2001).

One danger in relation to practice is highlighted by Hughes et al. (2014, p. 4) whereby:

> ... increasing policy emphasis on targeted, intensive interventions, shaped by a 'deficit' model of youth ... has become normalised through the language required of practitioners to support (increasingly competitive) funding bids.

Practitioners are increasingly under pressure to label people in one way or another to secure resources for CYW projects. This creates contradictions between promoting equality and acceptance of all, regardless of circumstances, and applying an arbitrary label in order to secure much needed funding support. While these contradictions are understandable they cannot be ignored as there is a danger that 'the problematising of behaviour is a tool to attract money' (Hughes et al., 2014, p. 4). We therefore urge that practitioners should critically question who the real beneficiaries of our work are and should continue to work with communities and young people to secure funding by alternative means.

In counteracting a pervasive pathology, we need to ingrain critical awareness of such discourse across practices that not only targets young people, but also involves communities of deprivation and migrant communities to name but a few. Otherwise, a pathologising discourse can become so embedded in social policy and public discourse that it becomes hegemonic. As an accepted or routine discourse, this pathology can be applied to discussion of whole sec-tions of our community in a deficit manner which perpetuates the hegemony and mitigates social change. Instead, we need to be careful that our response is not one that seeks to 'put people back on the right path' given that the notion of there being a right or wrong path for individuals assumes that there is a dominant, pre-set process which people should follow in order to be com-pliant and suitable humans.

Therefore, one practical strategy is that our practice needs to refrain from beginning from a deficit, pathogenic starting point and rather should start from a salutogenic perspective (Antonovsky, 1996) which focuses on posi-tivity and the possibility of collective action for change. In starting from a positive perspective and being critical of the deficits approach we can also begin to question who benefits from our practice. This assists in becoming critically aware of programmes which are tokenistic in involving participants without any power analysis or negotiation in regard to their participation or engagement in the programme and its purpose.

Real Beneficiaries

It seems fairly straightforward, to assert that the beneficiaries of our work are those we seek to engage with, work for, or those we support to facilitate learning and development in practice. However, as noted throughout this book, in the context of shrinking budgets, competitive tendering for resources and an under-mining of our practice, that there is a danger of becoming so complicit in striving for resources that the beneficiaries of our practice becomes blurred. Practitioners have, for many years, refined their capacity to 'play the game' in order to secure funding, and to develop expertise in finding dual-purpose resources—in meeting funder expectations whilst also utilising them to address the needs and aspira-tions of the community in which they work. The conception of 'in and against the state' (London Edinburgh Weekend Return Group, 1980) may be as relevant now as it was in 1980. As Shaw (2011) has highlighted in relation to community development, there is a danger that as opposed to critiquing the structural, often bureaucratic, managerialist way of working, we subscribe to it, which leads to an uncritical, 'one size fits all' approach to community engagement.

However, managing to work in a manner that critiques and challenges state ideology and deficit policy discourses could offer a catalyst for change. As Moodie (2013, p. 6) notes:

... the incorporation of community development by the state could be seen positively as part of a process of bottom-up pressure on the state, not just as a negative result of neoliberalism.

This is a tricky balance which requires critical consciousness and the use of emancipatory critical reflexive praxis to ensure that our practice is not subsumed by neoliberal discourse which effectively makes the state the beneficiaries of practice as opposed to those we work with.

As noted earlier, the articulation of the 'primary client' (Sercombe, 2010) for youth work practice ensures that identification of the beneficiary of practice may seem straightforward. However, this needs to be continuously reflected upon to ensure that there is not a tokenistic involvement with young people where in actuality there are often more subtle hegemonies at play, which create hidden agendas and uncritical nudging into further oppressive systems. Moreover, in relation to community development the 'primary client' is somewhat harder to decipher. There needs to be a recognition of multiple voices in striving for collective broader rights for communities whilst ensuring that the individual is not silenced within the process (Gormally, 2012). There is also the need to be a 'critical friend' (Gormally, 2012) to question and challenge why some voices are not apparent around the table. This process can ensure that there is no exclusion of members of a particular community and that the views of all those impacted by policy decisions are taken into account, and are campaigned on, to ensure they are the 'real beneficiaries'.

Of course, having multiple beneficiaries is not problematic providing that the practice has at its heart the interests of those we seek to work alongside. There is a danger that a culture of work becomes ingrained within a particular organisation or project. A kind of organisational cultural hegemony can create reliance on a specific organisation rather than promoting empowerment and self-advocacy. Within this context the practitioner feels responsible for the people they work with and potentially builds up a mutually reinforcing dependence resulting in an undermining of the social change focus of our practice. For real social change to happen people need to take ownership of their own learning but this cannot happen overnight nor will it happen if practitioners build up a culture of dependency on a particular project or organisation.

By asking these critical questions of our own practice, we can guard against and prevent ourselves from engaging in tokenistic endeavours. We can ensure that we are critically aware of the power dynamics that exist in societal structures and can engage with meaningful activism (see Chapter 5 for a discussion on power and activism) for the causes of social justice and equality.

Conclusion

This chapter has sought to highlight the context in which CYW practitioners currently operate. It provides an overview of how the patriarchal, neo-liberal, capitalist agenda individualises and marketises people and practices. Having set this context, the chapter has provided our vision for the future and then articulates four key areas for practitioners to explore in defining their own vision for practice. These areas highlight questions about what others want from our practice. They attempt to redirect our focus in challenging broader societal structures that maintain oppression and prevent us from subscribing to these detrimental practices. The critical process of thinking about the context of our practice, why we do this work, who do we work for and who benefits from our practice should ensure that we do not subscribe to a pathologising discourse that results in perpetuating power imbalances and injustices.

The chapter argues that as community and youth work practitioners we can engage in sociologically driven practices that aspire towards the creation of a more equitable and socially just society. It argues that by being critically conscious of our context and practice we can identify and attempt to address structural disadvantage, discrimination and inequality. This is done through refocusing on meaningful participation, deciphering collective rights, and awareness of broader political processes. The next chapter offers psychological perspectives on practice and in particular focusses on the ways that we can build strength in our quest for equality and social justice.

Bibliography

Abramovitz, M. and Zelnick, J. (2010). Double jeopardy: The impact of neoliberalism on care workers in the United States and South Africa. *International Journal of Health Services*, 40(1), 97–117.

Anotonovsky, A. (1996). The salutogenic model as a theory to guide health promotion. *Health Promotion International*, 11, 11–18.

Ball, S. J. (2013). *Foucault, Power and Education*. New York: Routledge.

Barber, T. (2007). Who is youth work for? Distortions and possibilities. *Scottish Youth Issues Journal*, 9, 77–88.

Beatty, C., Foden, M., McCarthy, L. and Reeve, K. (2015). *Benefit Sanctions and Homelessness: A Scoping Report*. London: Crisis.

Bello, W. (2002). *Deglobalization: Ideas for a New World Economy*. London and New York: Zed Books.

Bessant, J. (2007). Not such a fair go: An audit of children's and young people's rights in Australia. *Scottish Youth Issues Journal*, 9, 41–56. Retrieved 15 February 2008 from http://www.youthlinkscotland.org/webs/245/documents/SYIJIss9.pdf

Brookfield, S. (2005). *The Power of Critical Theory for Adult Learning and Teaching*. Berkshire: Open University Press.

Clarke, J. (2009). What's the problem? Precarious youth: Marginalisation, criminalisation and racialisation. *Social Work & Society*, 6(2), 306–314, www.socwork.net/sws/article/download/62/122, accessed 16 January 2015.

Coburn, A. and Gormally, S. (forthcoming). Youth work as emancipatory practice: Aspects of power, risk and resilience in equality work. *Journal of Youth Studies*.

Cooper, C., Gormally, S. and Hughes, G. (Eds.). (2015). *Socially-Just, Radical Alternatives for Education and Youth Work Practice: Re-Imagining Ways of Working with Young People*. Basingstoke: Palgrave MacMillan.

Cooper, C. (2010). Responding to unhappy childhoods in the UK: Enhancing young people's "well-being" through participatory action research. In I. Greener, C. Holden and M. Kilkey (Eds.), *Social Policy Review 22: Analysis and Debate in Social Policy*. Bristol: Policy Press.

Cooper, C. (2012). Imagining 'radical' youth work possibilities—Challenging the 'symbolic violence' within the mainstream tradition in contemporary state-led youth work practice in England. *Journal of Youth Studies* 15(1): 2012, 53–71.

De St Croix, T. (2010). Youth work and the surveillance state. In J. Batsleer and B. Davies (Eds.), *What Is Youth Work?* (pp. 140–152). Exeter: Learning Matters.

Giroux, H.(2016) *Dangerous Thinking in the age of new authoritarianism*. Oxon, Routledge

Giroux, H. (2014). No bailouts for youth: Broken promises and dashed hopes. In A. Ibrahim and S Steinberg (Eds.), *Critical Youth Studies Reader* (pp. 97–103). New York: Peter Lang.

Giroux, H. (2013). *Youth in Revolt: Reclaiming a Democratic Future*. Boulder: Paradigm Publishers.

Gormally, S. (2012). A social justice approach to community development. *The Irish Journal of Community Work*, Issue 3.

Gramsci, A. (1971). *Selections from the Prison Notebooks of Antonio Gramsci*. New York: International Publishers.

Hamilton, C. and Seymour, M. (2006). ASBOs and behaviour orders: Institutionalized Intolerance of Youth? *Youth Studies Ireland*, 1(1), 61–76.

Hallsworth, S. and Young, T. (2008). Gang talk and gang talkers: A critique. *Crime, Media, Culture: An International Journal*, 4(2), 175–195.

Hughes, G., Cooper, C., Gormally, S. and Rippingale, J. (2014). The state of youth work in austerity England—Reclaiming the ability to 'care.' *Youth and Policy*, 113, 1–14.

Knight, B. (2015). *The Society We Want*. Webb Memorial Trust. London: Alliance Publishing Trust.

Ledwith, M. (2011). *Community Development: A Critical Approach*. Bristol: The Policy Press.

London Edinburgh Weekend Return Group (1980). *In and Against the State* (2nd Ed.). London: Pluto Press.

Marx, K. and Engels, F. (1888, 2004). *The Communist Manifesto*. London: Penguin Classics.

Morgan, T. and O'Hare, B. (2001). The excluded adolescent: An exploration of the issues surrounding marginalised young people in Northern Ireland. *Scottish Youth Issues Journal*, 3, 49–68.

Moodie, V. (2013). To what extent does the 'In and Against The State' argument remain relevant? *Concept*, 4(3), 1–10.

Murray, C. (1996). *Charles Murray and the Underclass: The Developing Debate*. London: The Institute of Economic Affairs Health and Welfare University.

Sen, A. (2009). *On Justice*. London: Palgrave.

Sercombe, H. (2010). *Youth Work Ethics*. London: Sage.

Shaw, M. (2011). Stuck in the middle? Community development, community engagement and the dangerous business of learning for democracy. *Community Development Journal*, 46(2), 128–146.

Standing, G. (2011). *The Precariat: The New Dangerous Class*. London: Bloomsbury Academic.

Ord, J. (2007). *Youth Work Practice—Creating an Authentic Curriculum in Work with Young People*. Dorset: Russell House Publishing.

Taylor, T. (2010). Defending democratic youth work. *Concept*, 1(2), 3–10.

Wallace, D. and Coburn, A. (2003). Space—The final frontier: An exploration of territoriality. *Scottish Youth Issues Journal*, 5, 73–92.

Young, J. (2007). *The Vertigo of Late Modernity*. London: SAGE Publications.

· 8 ·

POSITIVE PSYCHOLOGY AND RESILIENCE IN COMMUNITIES

Introduction

This chapter considers psychological perspectives on how people can build strengths and improve their sense of well-being in order to help them prepare for, and take forward, the struggles they face in striving for equality and social justice. Drawing on ideas from positive psychology, the chapter examines how community resilience can be a driver of emancipatory practice. It also critiques how this kind of work impacts on workers and their relationships with employers and with people in communities. The chapter shows how combining positivity with existing practices can help guard against becoming complicit in maintaining the status quo.

In striving for a more socially just society where people are valued as full citizens who experience a good quality of life, community practitioners need to move beyond analysis of individual capacities that are heavily linked to development of interventionist strategies that seek to 'fix' individual deficiencies or behaviour that is identified as problematic. Sen (1985) has suggested that quality of life is linked to an individual's capacity to function well, and should not be restricted by a limited set of functions that are within reach. Rather, quality of life is linked to the capability of each person to have 'the freedom to achieve well-being' (Sen, 1985, p. 200). Similarly, Nussbaum (2000; 2003) has argued that every person should have the capability to function well and to achieve a good life. However, rather than being about individual abilities, Nussbaum suggests that the capacity to function well is about the value of freedom for all, so that everyone has the capability to flourish. This is consistent with Baker et al. (2004) in asserting a need for social change in order to bring about the conditions for equality.

In positive psychology the role of positive emotions, such as joy, love, contentment and interest, are suggested as a vehicle for broadening and building creativity and establishing a repertoire of reserved coping strategies that can be drawn on when needed (Fredrickson, 2001). For example, drawing on Izard (1997), Fredrickson (2001 p. 220) suggests contentment as a positive emotion, 'that broadens by creating the urge to savour current life circumstances and integrate these circumstances into new views of self and of the world'. According to Fredrickson (2001), positive emotion builds psychological resilience so that individuals not only feel good about themselves at the present time but it also increases the chance of their feeling good in the future. Yet, beyond the level of individual positivity for well-being, a growing interest in the relationship between happiness and well-being, also suggests that happiness has been underestimated, in terms of its function in sustaining communities and significantly improving well-being (Layard, 2003).

Increasingly our understanding of how individuals, communities and societies flourish, is useful in framing CYW practice around positive psychology which recognises, 'that people and experiences are embedded in a social context' (Seligman and Csikszentmihalyi, 2000), and where feelings of isolation prevail because we are intimate with fewer individuals and feel alienated (Seligman and Csikszentmihalyi, 2000).

Thus, improved wellbeing or quality of life can impact on both individual and social contexts that, when usefully combined in youth and community work practices can develop optimal learning. In this way practice encourages positive mental health and an emotionally secure identity in people and communities that have been 'pathologised out' of the kind of life they should be entitled to in terms of their Human Rights. Community and Youth Work (CYW) practice could assist in facilitating the achievement of circumstances and ways of knowing that are more socially just.

The Context for Youth and Community Work

As community practitioners, it is helpful to engage in practices that focus on positive emotions and promote human flourishing rather than to focus on deficiencies that lead to people languishing in a context where social change becomes difficult. CYW offers potential for an alternative discourse where people are valued as assets in communities that thrive, despite exceptional circumstances. In this sense the concept of resilience is useful in offering, 'flexibility in response to changing situational demands, and the ability to bounce back from negative emotional experiences' (Tugade et al., 2004, p. 1169).

Positive emotions contribute to conceptualisations of emancipatory practice, whereby the building of strengths and resilience can be developed as a means of enhancing collective capabilities for challenging oppressive structures—building community resilience, as distinct from individual resilience, integrates people, helping them to participate more fully in development of their communities. For example, in a study of youth gangs, the local community and broader society were found to have a role in providing opportunities and space for identity-enhancement among young people as opposed to excluding and dismissing them as 'nearly' citizens (Gormally, 2015).

Similarly, research into the experiences of independent care giving (Coburn and Wallace, 2012) highlighted that, rather than setting clear boundaries that prevented caring from taking over their lives, hidden carers became engulfed in their caring role, to the detriment of their own resilience (Twigg and Atkin, 1994, as cited in Coburn and Wallace, 2012). However, this research on carers experiences also showed that in taking a community development approach, independent care-givers could take increased control of their own lives. Instead of focusing on problems or deficiencies, it was important to build on people's existing assets in order to develop capacities and capabilities that facilitated strength and resilience in individuals, communities and organizations as a means to improve the wellbeing of the cared for, and the care-giver.

Further, at individual and social levels, there is a longstanding tradition of volunteering and engagement in youth and community work in order to facilitate change. Initially volunteering offers an altruistic opportunity to reciprocate a kindness, where people who have been 'helped' want to 'give something back' to their community, or to prevent others from repeating their mistakes. Yet, volunteering also creates capacity for people to renegotiate their social and personal relationships in areas such as governance or in taking on citizenship roles, which, according to Dinham (2007, p. 181), suggests a direct relationship between deep participation and feelings of well-being.

Research has shown that volunteer work is beneficial both for the community within which it takes place and for the volunteers (Dekker and Halman, 2003; Piliavin, 2003; Wilson and Musick, 2000). This can be explained with reference to a range of intrinsic and extrinsic rewards that map closely with three core components of resilience in terms of capacity to:

- act and adapt to changing circumstances;
- bounce back from adversity; and
- interact with others and take collective action.

As rewards for time given freely to a cause or to help others, volunteering has resilience enhancing potential for both individuals and communities. Through processes that build resilience as an important aspect of youth and community work praxis, resilience can thus be utilised to challenge oppression, whilst also striving for social change, this offers an alternative discourse to the further marginalising of people based on arbitrary distinctions in personal circumstances. Yet, resilience does not come without tension. Practitioners can be troubled by contexts in which they are employed to build the kind of resilience that is reduced to an individual deficiency-fixing level. As part of a pathological discourse embedded across western culture, the default position is to blame individuals for negative behaviours, rather than to ask why such behaviours persist and what needs to change in the world, in order for everyone to flourish. The next section considers the troubles and tensions that workers face in building resilience in communities and among themselves.

The Trouble with Risk and Resilience

In taking a human rights approach to promoting equality in community and social practices, Thompson (2003) suggests that discrimination operates at three levels. On a personal level, people make micro-level judgements about each other, often on grounds of belief or stereotyping and an individual may be discriminated against because of beliefs held by them, or by others about a particular kind of person. Yet, it is extremely difficult, perhaps impossible in current times, for an individual to exist outside of the culture in which they live. Thus, Thomson also identifies that discrimination on a cultural level is grounded in the norms, languages and symbols that people use to make sense of, and convey, their world. These norms languages and symbols can be passed on in subtle ways that help to maintain discrimination from one generation to the next. Finally, Thompson argues that personal and cultural discrimination are also impacted by macro-level structural factors relating to social divisions, such as class, race and gender, and factors relating to political and individual power relations.

Resilience is routinely described as the individualised capacity to deal with problems, as distinct from facilitating consciousness to challenge their root cause. Yet, the prevalence of a patholgising discourse and cultural context, calls into question the capacity of people to challenge their being labelled as at risk, risk-taking, problematic or in need of fixing. Historically, this has meant that, a position of resistance has often been seen as the starting point for challenging or changing contexts and circumstances of oppression. Most notably, during world war two, the resistance movement played a significant role in defeating Nazi oppressors. More recently, social movements, campaigns and specific acts of resistance have contributed to improving or changing conditions among individuals or for groups of people or communities who are oppressed or whose human rights are violated.

While acknowledging the vital role of resistance to circumstances of oppression and inequality, as it exists in our current world, conceptually we are troubled by the inherent position of the resistor, as a victim of powerful oppression, albeit one where resistance reclaims the position as one of powerful victim, the dominant power remains with the oppressor. We recognise this position as a useful mobiliser of community and individual action, where victim(s) fight back or work against the oppressor in order to challenge and change the world. Yet, this position sits uncomfortably with our analysis of power in which we aspire towards a power sharing relationship that strives for equality and social justice. So, in addition to resistance as a sociological response to oppression, we believe it is important to consider how the development of resilience might offer a means of challenging inequality and injustice, as part of an emancipatory methodology.

In considering this methodology, it is important to critique the building of resilience within the context of empowering practice. Individual resilience is utilised by many professions as a means to understanding how some people 'cope' in certain circumstances whilst others do not. The building of 'personal resilience' has been highlighted in the United Kingdom through a report following a series of riots (Communities and Victims Panel, 2012, p. 49) where it was suggested that:

> Every young person has they own story but one of the critical factors at play is individual strength of character. The Panel has heard evidence which, together, compromise character. These attributes include self-discipline, application, the ability to deter gratification and resilience in recovering from setback. This set of attributes may be collectively described using a variety of terms, including personal resilience or 'grit'. The Panel will use the term 'character,' as we feel it best covers the collective positive characteristics we discuss here.

This focus on individual character suggests that analysis of personal resilience is couched in a discourse of blame, of individual responsibility and of putting up with the structural problems which persist within society. Despite recognising the environment of austerity, the aim of striving for 'strong character' implies an individualistic response to problems. Moreover, it implies a flaw in the character of the individual that leads them to either engage in certain activities or to be unable to 'bounce back' quickly enough. For resilience to occur there must first be adversity or a high-risk situation or threat followed by the adaption to this experience (Ferguson et al., 2013). However, doing well, recovering and coping by overcoming the odds (Stein, 2005) often fails to question why the odds are stacked as they are.

In contrast to this, youth and community work practice facilitate engagement of individuals in collective activity, to build capacities and skills in a number of contexts. Resilience then is not one dimensional but rather there are multiple contexts and multiple resiliencies apparent (Ungar, 2004). Ungar (2004) notes that a focus on resilience can be salutogenic as opposed to pathogenic by focussing on the capabilities of individuals. Pooley and Cohen (2010) also note that the move towards analysing resilience is one of moving from the 'glass half empty' to the 'glass half full' as an approach to service provision.

Developing a focus on what facilitates wellbeing, Antonovsky (1979) considered sense of coherence (SOC), which is the capacity to make sense of the world and to feel confident that things will work out OK, as a means of understanding why people respond differently to adversity and are more or less likely to be affected by stressful situations. Where life is coherent and makes sense, and people feel that they can manage or meet the demands they face, they can meaningfully commit to making a life that works well. Where life is incoherent and chaotic people feel unsure of what to commit to and how to manage or meet the demands of life and thus, are more likely to experience stress or feel unable to manage their lives. It has also been noted that, 'sense of coherence has been linked to high associations with wellbeing and life satisfaction, reduced fatigue and loneliness' (Hefferon and Boniwell, 2011, p. 119).

This leads us to suggest that community work may be aligned with work on salutogenesis (Antonovsky, 1996) that is focused on the generation of good health and well-being, as distinct from pathogenesis, which is focused on the generation of disease. In taking a salutogenic perspective, community work practitioners' see people and communities in a positive light, starting where people are starting, by engaging with each other in conversational dialogue as a catalyst for learning. Our learning relationships are premised on an understanding that those who have otherwise been subject to oppression, for example, through negative stereotyping and discrimination, are partners in the learning process who bring their own assets to the table, and who are able to make a positive contribution to community life. This offers an alternative to the kind of contemporary pathological and discriminating discourses that take a position that is aligned to what Freire (1996) would call cultural invaders, people from outside of the community or learner experience who come in to sort or change things—because they know best, and so determine what is to be learned and how, where and why things happen!

Yet, in terms of building of resilience, there is debate on whether it is a process or an outcome (Ahern, Ark and Byers, 2008). Rutter (2007, p. 2) argues 'Essentially, resilience is an interactive concept that is concerned with the combination of serious risk experiences and a relatively positive psychological outcome despite those experiences'. However, the environment in which people in communities have to deal with serious risk experiences due to inequality or discrimination must also be challenged. Despite the recognition that individuals respond differently to difficult contexts (Rutter, 2007), we suggest that engaging communities in analysis of the structural as well as cultural factors, which give rise to the injustices they experience, is important as opposed to solely focussing on their capacity to adapt to the discriminatory situations they encounter. As Ungar (2008, p. 225) notes when adopting an ecological approach:

> ... resilience is both the capacity of individuals to navigate their way to health-sustaining resources, including opportunities to experience feelings of well-being, and a condition of the individual family, community and culture to provide these health resources and experiences in culturally meaningful ways.

In this sense, building resilience is always a dual process that takes place amidst the wider context of conditions that exist within family, community and culture. Building resilience involves parallel processes of developing individual and social strengths in order to create possibilities for culturally meaningful ways of being resilient. In this way, youth and community participation and engagement processes offer a counter hegemony to discourse that otherwise maintains a discriminating status quo. This is applied in community work terms when individual participants become stronger and more resilient because of their experiences of practice but when working in association with others, and over time, this strength and resilience can also become a catalyst for wider social change.

For example, the meaning of the youth council, and what it means to be a youth councillor, a youth exchange participant or to engage in a youth project, is co-constructed through dialogue between young people and youth workers. Similarly, the meaning and purpose of a campaign against local school closure, participation in an adult literacy class, outdoor education or parental reading group can be developed through collaborative critical conversations among adults and community practitioners.

Yet, our assertion is that, whatever the context for engagement, the processes of community work are located in helping people to make sense of the world in order to understand it and bring meaning to their lives. This is consistent with core elements of practice that aim to build confidence and facilitate empowerment and the achievement of full potential. Each of the above learning contexts engage in dialogical processes that can facilitate learning, confidence building and self-efficacy particularly in relation to personal capability (Bandura, 1997; Carr, 2011). Yet, this dialogue often happens in groups where, encouraging people to read the world differently facilitates their commitment to change in order to make a life that works well. While this brings individual and beneficial change for those who engage in youth and community work contexts, when developed in synthesis with each other and with wider social groupings, the cumulative effect of individual strengths, bring benefits for the whole community.

Peterson and Seligman (2004) identified a classification of twenty-four character strengths in order to understand how people are able to adapt to adverse situations or to help people to identify their 'signature strengths' as areas in which they can do well, feel very comfortable in, and so can be applied in pursuit of a meaningful and good life. These strengths were organised into six virtues, as noted in figure 5. In thinking about how these virtues might usefully be applied in CYW contexts, we build on the work of Peterson and Seligman (2004) to propose the following alignment to emancipatory purpose.

Virtues	Meaning	Emancipatory Purpose
Wisdom	The acquisition of knowledge	Knowing how power operates in society
Courage	Exercising of free will to accomplish goals, despite internal or external oppression	Believing that equality and social justice is possible
Love, humanity	Interpersonal strengths	Connecting in solidarity with others
Justice	Civic participation	Championing equality and social justice
Temperance	A buffer against excesses	Understanding that a good life does not mean the same life, it means the same chance to choose a particular kind of life
Transcendence	Connecting us to the wider universe	Pushing beyond the constraints of current experience to discover or create, as yet unknown, possibilities

Figure 5. Virtues aligning to emancipatory practice.

We believe that CYW practitioners can commit to developing capacity and a positive disposition that creates purpose and increases possibilities for cumulative community-wide social change. This alignment between salutogenic perspectives and resilience, offers an alternative perspective to the routine sociological and psychological theories that have underpinned development of community and emancipatory practices. Previously, effort was focussed on consideration of what was wrong with the world, exemplified in studies of delinquency, poverty and experiences of inequality, yet the emergence of positive psychology offers a focus on discovering how people thrive and flourish in order to promote what we can all do, to make our lives more meaningful and enjoyable. This is not an either or duality. Rather it brings into balance positive and negative factors that impact on lives that are possible but not always visible. It helps us to focus on how we can add purpose and meaning, not only as a way of coping with adversity and oppression, or of being content with the cards we have been dealt, but as a means of building strengths that help us to achieve our goals, to take forward social change, and to flourish. Of course, financial, family and social or cultural circumstances are important factors in shaping our individual experiences and we are not suggesting that positivity overrides poverty, but we do see possibilities for positivity and salutogenesis in practices that seek to illuminate and challenge social injustices such as poverty, in order to build strengths and take action for social change.

For example, in a study of how young people learned about equality, participation in an international youth exchange offered knowledge of power sharing relationships between adult youth workers and young people that were inextricably connected but not fixed. Instead, the process of decision taking followed ritualistic to-ing and fro-ing, over a prolonged period of negotiation, during planning meetings, residential work and the actual exchange itself, which led to shared construction of ideas and created new ways of working together. These negotiations appeared as mutually beneficial: young people were empowered to take important decisions; youth workers were empowered to practice critical youth work that facilitated change in power relations and development of more collaborative and cooperative relationships (Coburn, 2011). In the same study, conversations in the café area, further exemplified the dialogical and empowering nature of youth work.

Yet, despite the turn towards positivity, Shaw and McCulloch (2009) assert that there remains, 'an unhealthy tendency towards psychologistic (increasingly genetic) explanations for ... individual behaviour ... [that] ... ignore the obvious truth that individual experience is always embedded in social structure' (p. 5) and suggest this truth as important in sustaining unequal social relationships. They go on to argue that such relationships are 'rendered invisible' by a focus on individual, rather than collective power. We therefore recognise that focussing on positive psychology alone could limit possibilities for social change which reinforces the idea of collective resistance as a useful concept.

In thinking about the emergence of power and emancipatory practices, Thompson (2003) suggests that theorising on how ideas about equality might be applied in social practices is in the early stage of development. Despite work on human and social rights, there appears to be limited development of participatory practices among young people. There are clear contradictions in practices that seek to both liberate and contain or control young people (Bessant, 2007; Coburn, 2011; Deuchar and Maitles, 2008; Englund et al., 2009). Thus, the idea of parallel processes of resistance and resilience being applied in community contexts may be useful in the development of emancipatory practice.

However, this is only one application of resilience that, given the prevalence of programmes that 'teach' resilience as a personal coping skill, some community practitioners would still tend to identify as difficult to reconcile alongside emancipatory practice. In advocating for resilience in emancipatory practice, it is important that critically conscious practitioners shift from a perceived or ascribed role as individual 'fixer' or 'information giver' towards a role in facilitating power-sharing for building strength and taking collective action. In this sense the purpose of youth work is not to change young people's behaviour that is identified as risky, rather, the purpose of youth work is about creating conditions through which group or collective resilience can thrive in order to mitigate risk and bring more widespread community benefits that facilitate action for social change.

Conclusion

Drawing on positive psychology, we assert the possibilities for a counter-narrative that is positive about communities and young people and is critical of discourses that routinely demonise, criminalise or stereotype. To create this counter-narrative we should avoid the kind of reductionist discourse that seeks to engage young people and adults in superficial 'activity' or 'employability' programmes as a filler of time, in order to change their behaviour, which is identified as risky, troublesome or antisocial. Starting where people are starting, we should seek to build on existing strengths and facilitate engagement in deeper learning. Taking a resilient position, based on their knowledge of their own signature strengths, people can make choices about changes they want to achieve in their lives. Rather than being persuaded via short term, quick fix, interventions, a range of methods can be used to facilitate building resilience as part of open and longer term educational practices that offer time and space for people to identify and develop strengths and to form social relationships that enhance their prospects for making a good life (Sen, 1985).

Bibliography

Ahern, N. R., Ark, P. and Byers, J. (2008). Resilience and coping strategies in adolescents. *Paediatric Nursing, 20*, 32–36.

Anotonovsky, A. (1996). The salutogenic model as a theory to guide health promotion. *Health Promotion International, 11*, 11–18.

Baker, J., Lynch, K., Cantillion, S. and Walsh, J. (2004). *Equality: From Theory to Action*. Basingstoke: Palgrave Macmillan.

Bandura, A. (1997). *Self-efficacy: The Exercise of Control*. New York: Freeman.

Bessant, J. (2007). Not such a fair go: An audit of children's and young people's rights in Australia. *Scottish Youth Issues Journal*, 9, 41–56. Retrieved 15 February 2008 from http://www.youthlinkscotland.org/webs/245/documents/SYIJIss9.pdf

Carr, A. (2011). *Positive Psychology: The Science of Happiness and Human Strengths* (2nd Ed.). Hove: Routledge.

Coburn, A. (2011). Building social and cultural capital through learning about equality in youth work. *Journal of Youth Studies*, 14(4), 475–491.

Coburn, A. (2011). Liberation or containment: Paradoxes in youth work as a catalyst for powerful learning. *Journal of Youth and Policy*, 106, 60–77.

Coburn, A. and Gormally, S. (2014). 'They know what you are going through': A service response to young people who have experienced the impact of domestic abuse. *The Journal of Youth Studies*, 15(5), 642–663.

Coburn, A. and Wallace, D. (2012). *Caring Together: New Horizons for Independent Carers and Informal Care-giving in Clydesdale*, Glasgow: University of Strathclyde.

Riots Communities and Victims Panel (2012). *After the Riots: The Final Report of the Riots Communities and Victims Panel*. London: RCVP.

Dekker, P. and Halman, L. (Eds.). (2003). *The Values of Volunteering: Cross-cultural Perspectives*. New York: Kluwer Academic/Plenum.

Deuchar, R. and Maitles, H. (2008). Education for citizenship. In T. Bryce and W. Humes (Eds.), *Scottish Education: Beyond Devolution* (3rd Ed.) (pp. 285–292). Edinburgh: Edinburgh University Press.

Dinham, A. (2007). Raising expectations or dashing hopes?: Well-being and participation in disadvantaged areas. *Community Development Journal*, 42(2), 181–183.

Englund, T., Quennerstedt, A. and Wahlström, N. (2009). Education as a human and a citizenship right—Parents' rights, children's rights, or …? The necessity of historical contextualization. *Journal of Human Rights*, 8(2), 133–138.

Ferguson, C., Harms, C., Pooley, J., Cohen, L. and Tomlinson, S. (2013). Crime prevention: The role of individual resilience within the family. *Psychiatry, Psychology and Law*, 20(3), 423–430.

Fredrickson, B. L. (2001). The role of positive emotions in positive psychology: The broaden-and-build theory of positive emotions. *American Psychologist*, 56(3), 218–226.

Freire, P. (1996). *Pedagogy of the Oppressed* (M.B. Ramos, Trans. 2nd ed.). London: Penguin.

Gormally, S. (2015). 'I've been there, done that …': A study of youth gang desistance. *Youth Justice*, 15(2), 148–165.

Heffron, K. and Boniwell, I. (2011). *Positive Psychology: Theory, Research and Applications*. Maidenhead: McGraw Hill, Oxford University Press.

Layard, R. (2003). Happiness: Has social science a clue? *Lionel Robbins Memorial Lectures*. London: London School of Economics.

Layard, R. (2006). Happiness and public policy: A challenge to the profession. *The Economic Journal*, 116, 24–33.

Nussbaum, M. C. (2000). *Women and Human Development: The Capabilities Approach*. Cambridge: Cambridge University Press.

Nussbaum, M. C. (2003). Capabilities as fundamental entitlements: Sen and social justice. *Feminist Economics*, 9(2/3), 33–59.

Peterson, C. and Seligman, M. (2004). *Character Strengths and Virtues: A Handbook and Classification*. New York: Oxford University Press.

Piliavin, J. A. (2003). Doing well by doing good: Benefits for the benefactor. In C. L. M. Keyes and J. Haidt (Eds.), *Flourishing: The Positive Personality and the Life Well Lived* (pp. 227–247). Washington, DC: American Psychological Association.

Pooley, J. and Cohen, L. (2010). Resilience: A definition in context. *The Australian Community Psychologist*, 22(1), 30–37.

Rutter, M. (2007). Resilience, competence, and coping. *Child Abuse and Neglect*, 31, 205–209.

Rutter, M. (2006). Implications of resilience concepts for scientific understanding. *Annals of the New York Academy of Sciences, Resilience in Children*, 1094, 1–12.

Seligman, M. E. P. and Csikszentmihalyi, M. (2000). Positive psychology: An introduction. *American Psychologist*, 55, 5–14.

Sen, A. (1985). Well-being, agency and freedom: The Dewey lectures 1984. *Journal of Philosophy*, 82, 169–221. Retrieved 10 January 2015 from http://www.freelogy.org/w/images/d/dc/Sen85.pdf

Shaw, M. and McCulloch, K. (2009). Hooligans or rebels? Thinking more critically about citizenship and young people. *Journal of Youth and Policy* (101), 5–14.

Stein, M. (2005). *Resilience and young people leaving Care: Overcoming the odds*. Research Report. York: Joseph Rowntree Foundation.

Thompson, N. (2003). *Promoting Equality: Challenging Discrimination and Oppression* (2nd Ed.). Basingstoke: Palgrave MacMillan.

Tugade, M. M., Fredrickson, B. L. and Fieldman Barrett, L. (2004). Psychological resilience and positive emotional granularity: Examining the benefits of positive emotions on coping and health. *Journal of Personality*, 72(6), 1161–1190.

Twigg, J. and Atkin, K. (1994). In A. Coburn and D. Wallace (2011). *Youth Work in Communities and Schools*. Edinburgh: Dunedin Press.

Ungar, M. (2008). Resilience across cultures. *The British Journal of Social Work*, 38, 218–235.

Ungar, M (2004). A constructionist discourse on resilience: Multiple contexts, multiple realities among at-risk children and youth. *Youth & Society*, 35, 341.

Wilson, J. and Musick M. A. (2000). The effects of volunteering on the volunteer. *Law and Contemporary Problems*, 62, 141–168.

· 9 ·

A CRITICAL BORDER PEDAGOGY
FOR PRAXIS

Introduction

This chapter begins by considering critical pedagogy as a means of engaging with communities in times of social change. Next, boundary crossing in community practices is discussed to show how this can facilitate learning about difference, which helps make visible historical aspects that persist in maintaining an oppressive status quo. The chapter draws on research examples to show how community and youth work (CYW) practitioners can work across social and cultural borders to enhance understanding of difference. This analysis reveals that emphasis on boundary crossing in border pedagogy can also raise awareness of commonality through the shared experiences of people who are routinely labelled on grounds of, for example, ability, age, gender, race, or sexual orientation. The application and challenges of border pedagogy in CYW are identified as a threshold concept (Land et al., 2005) for sustainable emancipatory praxis in order to challenge the neoliberal project and contribute to the creation of possibilities for an alternative world.

Giroux (2005) defines educators, as teachers and cultural workers engaged in the construction of socially contextualised knowledge as distinct from being engaged in the transmission of abstract knowledge. When applied in a CYW context, this can be useful in working with adults and young people who seek to challenge and change communities in order to develop capabilities for equality and social justice. Asserting that community and youth workers are also cultural workers engaged in developing new knowledge across a range of social contexts is, we believe, foundational to understanding and responding to the world we currently occupy – where change is ever present and people are becoming increasingly aware of the flaws in the pervasive neoliberal capitalist system.

As the free market goes into overdrive, CYW practitioners are working on a day-to-day basis with people and communities who, at micro levels, are beginning to reclaim their power and to reassert equality and social justice as having primacy over profit. These early stirrings of concern are already bringing some macro level moments of unrest across the world. For example, the occupy movement challenges neoliberal capitalism and austerity, and seeks to raise awareness of how and why political elites seek to sustain multi-national corporations over sustainable communities. In doing so, ordinary people engage in dialogue about the possibilities for an alternative worldview. When people make sense of what is happening and begin to see or believe that an alternative to neoliberalism is possible, then social change becomes doable.

Rather than accepting the current system as the only way possible, throughout this book we have considered questions and exemplified practices that have been useful in CYW contexts and in challenging the status quo. It is in this sense that border pedagogy is identified as a threshold concept (Land et al., 2005) in conceptualising community and youth work as an emancipatory praxis for an alternative and sustainable future that contributes to the current impetus for social change. We see this as an emerging professional disciplinary area that is finding its way in taking forward the struggle for equality and social justice.

Starting Where People Are with Critical Pedagogy

Throughout this book we have articulated an emancipatory vision for practice. This vision is grounded in the creation of a resilient community of practice, which is emancipatory in undertaking a critical analysis of power in the face of negative hegemonic norms that would otherwise maintain the status quo in favour of oppressive neo-liberalism. Seeking to challenge the inequalities that exist and are ingrained in corporate culture, the nature and purpose of CYW means that it can be identified as a practice for freedom which challenges the status quo.

Yet, we have also shown that it can also be regarded as a practice of compliance that socialises people into neo-liberalism by increasingly pushing them towards a more compliant regime. This includes the adaptation of developmental grassroots processes for use in practice that meets the requirements of a creeping neoliberalism in seeking outcome driven targets in terms of policy on employability, good parenting and behaviour management.

Starting where people are, not where someone else thinks they should be, offers a useful starting point for critical educational methodologies. This promotes that 'teaching is a creative act, a critical act and not a mechanical one … [where] … the curiosity of the teacher and the students, in action, meet on the basis of teaching-learning' (Freire, 2007, p. 68). This shows 'respect for the knowledge of living experience … for popular knowledge … for cultural context' (Freire, 2007, p. 72) and accordingly, starting from their concrete everyday experience helps to ensure that learners or community change-makers are able to engage in critical dialogue about their existing knowledge of the world and become critically conscious to their localised power. By widening horizons to another world-view, new knowledge can be generated as a counterbalance to the subtle hegemonic neoliberal messages that inform and drive contemporary capitalist societies.

As problem posing, critical pedagogy identifies education as a means of producing identities that are constructed in response to different, or alternative, forms of knowledge and power. The aim of the critical educator is to work co-operatively and in partnership with people who are oppressed to question and challenge the status quo and the systems that sustain current power structures, which perpetuate privilege among those who are already powerful. Community and youth work practitioners need to understand the ways in which those systems operate in order to make visible the social, cultural and political constructions of power that require to be challenged if social change is to be facilitated. Yet, it is not enough for practitioners to know and understand such things, as solely having awareness brings no impetus for change. It is only when action happens, in full partnership with the communities that we work alongside, that change happens. Indeed for change to be sustainable, the power balance in such partnerships must be overtly tipped towards people who are oppressed, rather than workers whose role it is to facilitate empowerment.

The nature of the negotiated power sharing relationships in CYW, as discussed in Chapter 5, is grounded in an activist methodology that creates realities in social and cultural contexts where conscientisation is the start of a political process for change. Bringing a theoretical understanding of how difference is constructed and sustained through powerful institutions that exist in education, media and political systems, and across the corporate world, is useful in creating possibilities for critical dialogue among communities that are impacted by oppressive constructions of difference.

In CYW, conversational (dialogical) education opens new lines of enquiry and frees up those involved from the manipulations of powerful others. Thus, seeing education as socially and politically contextualised means that:

> Critical pedagogy needs to create new forms of knowledge through its emphasis on breaking down disciplinary boundaries and creating new spheres in which knowledge can be produced ... [and] ... starts with the everyday and the particular as a basis for learning.
>
> Giroux (2005, p. 69)

In this way, to be a community educator is also to be a social and cultural worker who is engaged holistically with the lived experiences of people in communities. Practice that is underpinned by critical pedagogical methodology, engages people in education by encouraging them to become inquisitive, to question why things are the way they are, and to pose problems through which learning, collaboration and resolution to problems can be found. While often argued as a means of radicalising or transforming school-based education (Giroux, 2005), we believe that operating informally and using dynamic and organic methods means that critical pedagogy is useful in working with all age groups and across a range of educational contexts. Critical pedagogy is applicable to informal and so-called radical community education and development contexts and offers a more open way of seeing the world which, once visible, can help to galvanise communities in the struggle for social justice.

Friere (1996) notes that 'banking education' fosters compliance with dominant ideas, knowledge and values. It perpetuates teaching from a position of hierarchical power relations between young people in schools and adults who, as school teachers, are often constrained by a subject driven curriculum, that is prescribed in order to pass exams and 'do well' in the labour market. Yet, we do not see critical pedagogy as a 'radical' alternative. We simply assert critical pedagogy as a way of thinking about education that is democratic and purposeful in reaching beyond labour market drivers in response to Sen's (1985) question about what makes a good life. Critical pedagogy is thus useful in the context of schooling and as a means of socialising people into a less compliant and more questioning way of engaging in education that is about thinking critically about the world we presently occupy and whether this facilitates a good life for everyone, or only those power elites and processes we have discussed earlier.

We also suggest critical pedagogy as the basis for practices that are consistent with Illich (1970) who proposed a de-schooling of society, in response to concerns that a school curriculum was associated with social ranking of people according to the certificates gained through instruction, and a system which assumes that most learning happens as a result of professional teaching in a particular setting.

In making this assertion, we reject the social construction of age as a means of organising either education or society, or indeed most other forms of social and cultural endeavour. We also reject the notion that 'traditional' or standardised forms of schooling offer the singular means of achieving a good life, and as noted in Chapter 1, that educational progress has succumbed to the neoliberal project and become complicit in maintaining the inequalities this brings. Instead, we affirm a social and democratic purpose for education, as discussed in Chapter 2, whereby a problem posing, critical pedagogy is consistent with the values and principles of educational methodologies that are overtly political and emancipatory and are not constrained by age or setting.

Unfortunately, for now, the dominant discourse in contemporary education remains power-laden and is often interpreted to mean school education, with educator meaning school teacher. This discourse ignores the possibility and positive contribution of community based adult education, community development and youth work in facilitating transformational change among people of all ages. It regards informal education as marginal or specialist activity.

Yet, being concerned by the 'hidden curriculum', beyond even the most obvious hegemony (Gramsci, 1999) that brands the poor and privileges the rich, Illich, writing in the 1970s, was most concerned with:

> This hidden curriculum of schooling ... [that] ... adds prejudice and guilt to the discrimination which a society practices against some of its members ... [and] ... serves as a ritual of initiation into a growth-orientated consumer society for rich and poor alike.
>
> Illich (1970, p. 33)

Illich's concerns about privileges in education are as important now, as they were in the 1970s. Illich proposed new goals for education that were not concerned with what someone should learn, rather, that education should be concerned with questioning 'What kinds of thing and people might learners want to be in contact with in order to learn' (Illich, 1970, p. 7). This is important in school based education and in a wider range of CYW education in community contexts. For example, in the school domain, a mix of people that is not limited to qualified school teachers is required in order to develop the kind of educational processes that assist young people to achieve their fullest potential and to engage in political discussion or process. In community contexts people can become critically conscious of the complex problems and challenges they encounter by engaging in purposeful dialogue as a starting point for the analysis of power that can lead to social change.

Involving community and youth work educators in schools and in other community and cultural contexts, is consistent with Freire (2005) who reminds us that, 'an educational practice in which there is no coherent relationship between what educators say and what they do is a disaster' (p. 97). For example, we have already raised concerns about the routine use of formulaic programmes in response to issues of employability or parenting, suggesting that these are strengthened by raising critical questions about the conditions in which such issues may be created or troublesome. This is entirely in keeping with those unifying values and principles discussed in Chapter 2, that seek to make visible the hidden knowns of practice and to place equality and social justice at the very heart of CYW praxis.

This area of concern for a growth-orientated consumer society has increased, beyond even the wildest dreams of Milton Freidman who, as an advisor to American President Regan and UK Prime Minister Thatcher, greatly influenced the unrestricted global advancement of the neo-liberal project in the 1980s. Thus, it is no accident that neoliberalism has taken hold as a destructive force against the creation of conditions for social and democratic purposes and in doing so, has halted progress in the struggle for equality and social justice.

Yet, the neoliberal project is not confined to sustaining inequality and injustice among the poorest communities. Its obsession with the free market as a means of promoting economic growth has led to increased concerns in regard to climate change, poverty and pollution with higher levels of unemployment, a widening of inequality, rising migration and social friction, whereby:

These problems all have the same basic cause – the desire for endless consumption growth without due concern for the effects on the environment and inequality … [where] … the desire to cut costs and boost short-term profits, driven by the demands of the financial markets, means that real wages have also been declining … [and] … the extreme free market model is also behind the rise in inequality.

Maxton and Randers (2016, p. 73)

In this sense, our struggle for emancipatory practice is not only about achieving a good life for all and creating a more socially just world – it is also an ecological struggle for survival and the capacity for future generations to also make good lives.

When we started writing this book our on-going calls to challenge the status quo in order to achieve social change were, for us, about a shift to the collective social purposes of the political left. Yet, by 2016, this call to challenge and change the status quo has been taken forward in the most spectacular and unexpected of ways. New political movements for social change have emerged through argument put forward by people utilising privileged positions in terms of corporate power, elite education and/or material wealth. For example, where others have failed to do so, people like Donald Trump and Nigel Farage, have convinced 'ordinary' people that change is possible and that contemporary democracy is not working effectively. Suggesting their way, of being tough on immigration and disparaging of people who are different, as the only real chance for change, their arguments have struck a chord with many who were previously disengaged. The seemingly anti-establishment and protest motive behind votes leading to Brexit and the election of President Trump has undoubtedly created social change but a change that seems to come from an 'othering' which has concretised the hardening of self in opposition to difference (Young, 2007).

As the inequalities and poverty that are associated with market driven capitalism and materialism advance, amid the continuation of oppressive experiences discussed in previous chapters, there has been a shift in focus from the social to the individual, from the democratic to the autocratic and from power-sharing to power-grabbing. For example, in the United Kingdom, a steady media-fuelled demonisation of European Law has portrayed this as an imposition of control from the EU's headquarters in Brussels over the will of the British people. Over time, this has created conditions which, at best, make invisible any progress that has been made (in terms of European employment and social rights) and at worst, is divisive in creating and sustaining cultural and ethnic stereotypes that generate tensions between groups.

While new political enlightenment is largely overdue, this initial reaction to mistakes that are perpetuated by increasingly disconnected political elites, seems to have galvanised the ultimate in protest votes. In order to challenge the status quo, the most politically disenfranchised have become mobilised in rejecting contemporary politics. Fuelled by often charismatic players who hide their own elite privileges or use of power, to appear as 'for the people', seems to have perpetuated a divisive 'us and them' narrative of caring for 'all of us' and taking action to sort out the 'other—them'. As a newly engaged electorate, such powerful narratives, aligned with an impulse for change, have persuaded people to vote for Brexit in the United Kingdom, and for Trump in the United States. This may actually add to existing tensions and threaten to dismantle progress that has been made in working towards equality or social justice that has been achieved in recent decades.

This new political rupture is not the same as Giroux's predictions about the promise of new social movements being formed to create, a 'politics that uncovers the harsh realities imposed by casino capitalism ... [to help in] ... establishing a society in which matters of justice and freedom are understood as the crucial foundation of a substantive democracy' (Giroux, 2013). However, this deviation from hopeful predictions lost through this ultimate protest vote, may only be temporary. Both Brexit and the Trump presidency may, in the longer term, facilitate political education and new ways of reading the world in order to change it and to reclaim democratic possibilities for equality and social justice for all.

Meantime, the recently engaged or re-engaged electorate has sent a signal to the world, that in the United Kingdom and United States at least, many people who do not routinely engage in political discussion, have emerged from a period of apathy, to assert that the current political system has failed them and they are looking for change. Although not all people who voted for Brexit or Trump are new voters, for some this is the first time they have engaged in political processes of decision making. Further, whether new or existing voters, they may not all be inclined to take action for social change. Thus, while we may not agree with the kind of political manoeuvring that has brought this new wave of political activism, it does exist, and it may bring renewed hopes for alternative forms of politics to emerge. For example, the 'Occupy' movement continues in raising awareness of the 1% of people who have a disproportionate share of wealth, and gains in the assertion of Human Rights have been useful in taking forward the struggle for equality. Yet, in themselves, these are not enough.

Consolidating words and deeds in ways that are authentic and trustworthy is important in creating spaces for critical conversations about difference, as part of an emancipatory practice which is:

> ... pedagogically safe and socially nurturing rather than authoritarian and infused with the suffocating smugness of a certain political correctness ... [as part of] ... a broader democratic politics of voice and difference.
>
> Giroux (2005, p. 25)

Yet, in identifying the hidden knowns of CYW practice (see Chapter 2), we have already noted that emancipatory praxis is largely hidden from funders and from people involved in policy development. So, making such critical questioning overt, and synthesising these ideas, could help CYW practitioners to encapsulate typical ideas about practice and delivery methods, while also embracing changing professional narratives about the meaning and theorising of emancipatory praxis.

Troubled by the constraints of a banking model of education, Freire (1970, 1996) suggested that, 'the more students work at storing the deposits entrusted to them, the less they develop the critical consciousness which would result from their intervention in the world as transformers of that world' (1996, p. 54). Banking education puts the teacher in control of what is learned, in a 'ready-to-wear approach ... [that] ... serves to obviate thinking' (Freire,1996, p. 57). As an alternative, Freire proposed a critical pedagogy that uses problem posing as the focal point for learning.

Drawing on Freirian pedagogy, authors such as Beck and Purcell (2010), Coburn and Wallace (2011), propose that youth and community work practice begins when people start to question the situations and realities they live in, and to see these as problematic. They suggest dialogue as much more than conversation and see it as a deliberate act of transformation. Further, they argue that new levels of consciousness are achieved as the relationship between those involved in the conversation is changed through dialogue and, as before, through a process of co-investigation which creates new knowledge. This idea of critical youth and community practice resonates with principles of 'social purpose education' (Martin, 2007, p. 10) which, in Scotland, has been aligned to democratic purpose and is characterised in the following terms:

- Participants/learners are treated as citizens and social actors.
- Curriculum reflects shared social and political interests.

- Knowledge is actively and purposefully constructed to advance collective interests.
- Pedagogy is based on dialogue rather than transmission.
- Critical understanding is linked to social action and political engagement.
- Education is always a key resource in the broader struggle for social change.

Martin (2007, p. 10)

Martin (2007) suggests a critical educational purpose for community work, that is grounded in 'nurturing the democratic impulse harnessed to a social justice agenda … [as] … our distinctive … 'vocation' in the sense of finding a meaning for life in the work we do' (p. 11). Martin highlights a need to challenge the status quo and 'to work against the grain of the neo-liberal common sense of our times' (p. 11) and in doing so resist contemporary discourses that work against democracy and social justice.

In this sense, work that is critical and educational includes the kind of youth work where young people are offered spaces to challenge inequalities and through dialogue and problem posing to change the status quo (Batsleer, 2008; Coburn, 2012). Similarly, critical adult education is not simply reduced to short courses that seek to improve employability or computing skills, but uses these as a catalyst for developmental processes of individual and collective empowerment. Critical CYW seeks to develop new possibilities for social and democratic practices that reach beyond basic activity or leisure time programmes as part of a community based and dissenting vocation (Martin, 2001).

Critical pedagogy helps to create conditions through which participants can produce new forms of knowledge or understanding by identifying and decoding societal norms and values to understand how symbols are used to make meaning (Cohen, 1985). This new knowledge and understanding can transform ideas and generate learning that enables people to see through hegemony to read the world, and themselves, differently (Freire, 1970; 1976; Giroux, 2005).

This different reading of the world involves people in challenging themselves and others, through critical dialogue and reflective thinking by working across existing boundaries of knowledge and practice, in order to see, hear and understand alternative interpretations and perspectives. Drawing on longitudinal research, the next section exemplifies how this kind of border crossing pedagogy can be developed in everyday CYW practice.

Creating Educational Borderlands That Can Assist in Learning About Equality

In becoming conscious, not only of the world and the way knowledge is produced but of our own capacities to produce new knowledge, and to change the world, we align with core elements of critical pedagogy (Giroux, 2005; Kincheloe, 2008; McLaren, 2009). At a micro level, problem-posing education can be pivotal in the formation of understanding about identity and cultural difference.

Research into youth work (Coburn 2012) found that an international exchange group was important in creating a safe 'borderland' for young people to consider their existing worldview and who they were becoming. For example, when asked about whether equality featured in youth work one young man called Craig, was involved in the youth exchange and talked about his experiences of meeting a group of young Muslims for the first time:

> You get to know people from different countries and different religions and everything … I had a lot of problems with like getting to know people and I didn't trust anybody that I didn't know. Then, through that … [youth exchange] … I just learned everybody's the same, never judge a book by its cover, d'you know what I mean?
>
> Craig

This international exchange, created a chance for Craig to meet young people that he perceived as different and whose beliefs and values were different to his own. In this way young people like Craig met Muslim young people through youth work. This mixing across cultural boundaries helped him to overcome problems of trust and to learn that despite any differences, such as those related to lifestyle or religion, there were commonalities:

> They were Muslim … it was totally different because er … it just makes you think … it's just the way you're perceiving them … it was good because we got to know a wee bit of their history … to like, learn about each other.
>
> Craig

Until then, Craig's opinion of Muslim young people and the Muslim religion was based on media reporting of the so-called 'war on terror'. Getting to know the young people behind his preconceptions prompted him to reflect on this view and to avoid prejudging people on the basis of what he could see or thought he knew about them.

Giroux (2005) suggests that when developing emancipatory practice, it is important to make colonial and other histories visible in order to reconfigure understanding of the world. Having learned about cultural and historical differences through the youth exchange, Craig could apply his understanding about difference to other aspects of his life now, and in future. Learning through involvement in the youth exchange impacted on Craig's conceptualization of difference inside and outside of the setting, and beyond the period of his participation in youth work.

Baker et al. (2004) have argued that by challenging cultural assumptions new ideas are produced which help people to reconsider their identities. Craig's response was typical of all young people involved in the youth exchange group and who described their experiences of it as life changing:

> It's been fantastic, a great experience ... I've met people that I'd never have met and ... I think we'll be friends for many years ... just because they came from different countries ... they're not really that different ... they all have their own hobbies ... we had some arguments over football and things like that ... but with everyone speaking different languages and using signs or broken English, it worked ... we found out about the way we live ... not tourist stuff ... but the way we all live ... our everyday stuff.
>
> Ryan

Again, despite language and cultural barriers, Ryan said the exchange helped him to find out about how young people lived in other countries and cultural contexts. By challenging his assumptions of difference, he was able to see commonality and suggested that the exchange reached beneath the surface of 'tourist stuff' to develop deeper understanding of difference. Thus, where youth exchanges encourage young people to experience culture and to learn about difference, new ideas and identities can be developed.

Experiencing everyday encounters of life, by participation in international exchange, young people could challenge cultural assumptions and create new understandings of their world. In youth exchange meetings and informal café conversations, the young people also talked about the exchanges and the people they met, or the processes of preparing for the exchange. Youth workers encouraged them to reflect on their historical constructions of identity and how they formed opinions about difference. Engaging in critical conversation before, during and after the exchange, enabled young people to make judgments about themselves and to consider how they might use their new understandings to shape their own identities and to consider how they could relate to people they encountered, who were not like them. In this setting, youth work offered a space that was somewhere between overt action for social change, and the maintenance of existing power relations, where the negotiation of programmes between youth workers and young people were sometimes adult led, but at other times appeared to be led by young people.

When talking about identity and youth culture, Ryan also reflected on how the exchange had changed his own perceptions:

> Everyone has their own morals and cultural identity ... young people have different views from adults, that comes with them having different experiences ... But it's not really about age ... its more your experiences ... like my experiences of culture have been changed because of my experiences in [exchange location].
>
> Ryan

Ryan understood his experiences of youth culture as part of a broader and changing cultural identity. Ryan was asked to consider what influenced those changes, not what his views became:

> I think time plays a part ... because countries change over time ... things change, laws change, people change ... so how you view something at one point in time changes ... as you change over time. You're views of culture and morals change, as you change ... who I am now is different from the person I was before the exchange.
>
> Ryan

Ryan identified contributory factors in how culture and identity were formed, and in how these might be socially constructed, inside or outside of the youth work setting. This analysis concluded that the international youth exchange offered possibilities for young people to learn about difference and also about themselves and their formation of identity.

Although specific to youth work, the international exchange exemplifies how CYW practice can assist adults and young people to explore boundaries and so experience and consider difference. The CYW setting becomes a site of transformation where:

- Social practices can create possibilities for learning through border crossing.
- The social construction of ideas can be questioned and through dialogue new ideas, meanings and understandings are generated.
- Learning across borders can be a catalyst for action and social change.

Coburn (2011, p. 33)

This suggests CYW as a border crossing pedagogy that brings capacity for collaboration between participants and developers of education as co-creators of new ideas by working through difference to create new knowledge. This may include working across professional borders, such as those between school and community, or between health, leisure and social work services, for example, work that seeks to improve people's social circumstances by envisioning an alternative to contemporary market driven economies, and their emotional and physical well-being (see Chapters 7 and 8). As a border crossing pedagogy CYW can also incorporate working across social and cultural borders such as those of class, gender or race, in the analysis of power relations or in fostering participation that enhances, and creates new ways of thinking about, and understanding, difference. It may also work across a bricolage of communities (as shown in Chapter 4) or across political interests to facilitate individual and collective action for social change. In this context, striking a balance between political priorities or contemporary social policy, and the wider educational possibilities for social change is pivotal to thinking about CYW as border pedagogy.

This kind of equality work is particularly important in a society that defines people who do not 'fit' within particular constructions of normality, or who are labelled as marginal or vulnerable to exclusion. Freire (1996) stated that people are never marginal or outside of society, that everyone is in society, but highlighted that some people are oppressed by the organisational and institutional structures they live within. Recognising the conditions in which such labels are applied and that these conditions are outwith the control of those identified as living in the margins of society, is a starting point for understanding that to integrate people into existing regimes of oppression does not change the systemic factors that have created inequality in the first place. An alternative and more critical pedagogy enables people to think about how the systems that oppress them might be transformed. Building on Giroux's theorising of border pedagogy (Giroux, 2005) offers insights into the challenges that a liberating pedagogy creates (see the following, Figure 6, for an outline of challenges that are present in theory and practice).

While this theory and its challenges resonate throughout this book and should come as no surprise to the reader, we do not believe that a 'big bang' theory will provide the impetus for repositioning professional CYW practice towards the purposes that are present in our analysis of 'hidden knowns' and to reclaim its emancipatory purpose (see Chapter 2). Seeing this as problematic, and given everything we have said about the historical and shifting nature of contemporary practice, as both seeking to challenge but at times becoming increasingly compliant with policy drivers that sit uncomfortably with our deepest values and principles, we believe that a subtler approach is needed if we are to work towards a renewed vision for practice. Instead we return to the

Theory for Border Pedagogy	Challenges for Critical Educators
Education should be reconstructed to make difference a central tenet of citizenship and democratic public life.	Shifting from a hierarchy of struggles and celebration of difference, to take the struggle for equality and justice into broader spheres of everyday life.
Conditions for cultural re-mapping as resistance to cultural dominance.	Crossing cultural borders in order to rewrite difference through analysis of power to reveal voices and narratives for new forms of culture and identity.
Identities are fragile and multi-faceted. Borderlands offer space for intermingled voices and experiences.	Critical analysis of multi-layered and contradictory ideologies as a source of experimentation, creativity and possibility.
Recognition of a duality of power—as historical and socially constructed domination and power analysis critical interrogation of difference.	Critical reading and analysis of power from a position of responsible authority as committed intellectuals.
Educational literacy engages learners in historical, social, contextual and oppositional readings of ideological and personal narratives.	Orthodoxies on power as dominant force for oppression and recognition of its purpose in creating a democratic society.
The curriculum needs restructuring to incorporate lived ideologies, traditions, communities and histories as important.	Synthesising lived experience with particular pedagogies that bring investment in cultural politics and reconstructed discourses of opposition and hope.

Figure 6. Challenges in Theory and Practice. Adapted from Giroux (2005, pp. 150–152).

work of Maxton and Randers (2016) who seek to promote sustainable social change in suggesting that:

> Rich-world nations will need to change their economic systems ... [and] ... step back from to-day's economic mantra, which promises individual freedom, applauds free markets and free trade, and minimises state influences, and instead rearrange their economies to boost average well-being.
>
> Maxton and Randers (2016, p. 4)

In considering how such radical ideas could happen overnight, Maxton and Randers (2016) suggest that doing nothing is not an option. They also propose that although it is possible to create change quickly, if enough people are mobilised to disrupt the status quo, the chance of a critical mass of people being inclined towards a revolutionary approach is not realistic, given the current neoliberal stronghold on social thought. Thus, they suggest a more gradual transition that changes enough to make a difference but keeps people largely on side, and only disrupts what needs to be disrupted in changing the status quo.

We believe that this kind of gradual change, has already been happening in CYW for some time, and so have recently proposed that border pedagogy can be offered as a threshold concept for shifting CYW practice closer towards its emancipatory core that is transformational and sustainable.

Border Pedagogy as a Threshold Concept for Community and Youth Work

Land, Meyer and Baillie (2010) argue that, just as passing through a doorway or 'portal' enables new perspectives to come into view, some concepts help us to take a step forward in seeing things differently. As a 'conceptual gateway' threshold concepts are identified as:

- Transformational—bringing a shift in perspective
- Integrative—exposing previously hidden connectivity
- Irreversible—unlikely to be forgotten or unlearned
- Troublesome—taking people out of their comfort zone, encountering the unknown
- Liminal/Transitional—crossing from partial understanding to a new way of being can be unsettling

Adapted from Land et al. (2010, pp. ix–x)

Land et al. (2010) assert that when operating in sub-liminal mode, practitioners experience a sense of loss and often reject new meanings in responding to shifting perspectives or troublesome ideas. This seems to resonate with contemporary debates in CYW. These include the extent to which engagement can still be called youth work if hidden knowns are compromised. For example, if young people have not freely chosen to attend, or if power and the practice of freedom are mitigated by funder determined outcomes and expectations?

They go on to state that their ideas resonate with theories of transformative learning and conceptualisations of disorientating dilemmas (Mezirow, 2009). However, they suggest a different starting point from Mezirow in asserting that learners must, 'be open to the possibility of transformation in the first place' (Land et al, 2010, p. xii). In this sense educational transformation is not something that happens passively and unconsciously, rather it is a conscious act of knowing and re-knowing.

Border pedagogy has already been suggested as a useful way of framing a conceptualisation of youth work (Coburn, 2010). Taking this as a threshold concept for CYW, it is possible to also conceptualise the possibility for youth work as education (Harland and McCready, 2012); as this methodology can be applied in a range of settings if hidden knowns are consciously critiqued. Making sense of the world and creating new meanings by working on boundaries in order to deconstruct inflexible borders, takes us outside of current discourse to create new ideas or alternative forms of knowledge (Giroux, 2005).

In this sense, we propose that border pedagogy can be useful in analysing and developing CYW practice. The sites in which we practice, the areas where we can raise consciousness, discuss existent knowledge and challenge the status quo can be expansive and are not necessarily limited to traditional settings. Thus we argue the need to:

- Re-engage in the kind of rigorous debate that opens up the possibility of alternative expressions of meaning (Boyd and Myers, 1988).
- Be receptive to the possibility for changed perspectives.
- Recognise that our established meanings or assertions may no longer be valid, and that we may feel the need to grieve this loss.

Adapted from Land et al. (2010)

We believe that internationally, our practice in a liminal state, defined as:

> A time when the old configurations of social reality are increasingly seen to be in jeopardy, but new alternatives are not yet in hand ... liminality is a safe place in which to host such ambiguity, to notice the tension and unresolved without pressure, but with freedom to see and test alternative textings of reality.
>
> Brueggemaan (1995, pp. 319–20)

We propose that border pedagogy offers a threshold concept which aids discussion regarding the future for CYW: where the unthinkable can be realised in new configurations of methodological praxis across a range of professional domains.

Future Challenges

This book has sought to explore how CYW can be a foundational practice for social change. We have explored and asserted the underpinning value of our practice as striving towards a more socially just and equal society. This has led to a discussion about what community is and how we can engage with people in different communities as a catalyst for social change. The connecting nature of community is viewed as a place to ignite positive social change, particularly where there is a deep understanding of the multiple power differentials apparent within, between and outwith communities that are engaged in local activity for change. Adopting an activist approach fuelled by consciousness of the dynamics in which we work will enable change. The feasibilities and possibilities of practice have further been discussed throughout the book. Although we have reached the end of this particular volume, we hope this is only the start of a conversation between CYW practitioners and across our bricolage of communities. We add to a broad literature on critical pedagogy in arguing that using this approach incorporates problem-posing dialogue, critical conversation and decoding of meaning, into the existing repertoire of resources and skills that people and practitioners can draw upon to learn about equality and social justice. Actively embracing our liminal state may feel precarious particularly given the current economic, social and political environment. However, we argue the need to start where we are at and to see this as an opportunity to collectively regroup in creating a counter discourse to the deficits-based, pathologising narrative that has gained momentum in some political spheres. Collective action, awareness of context, holding those who need to be as accountable, and striving for a better world, means our future challenges are vast, but hopefully, not insurmountable. In this sense, we end on a note of optimism in the capabilities for people and practitioners to work together in order to achieve the kind of social change that is needed for improved equality and social justice.

References

Baker, J., Lynch, K., Cantillion, S. and Walsh, J. (2004). *Equality: From Theory to Action*. Basingstoke: Palgrave Macmillan.

Batsleer, J. (2008). *Informal Learning in Youth Work*. London: Sage.

Beck, D. and Purcell, R. (2010). *Popular Education Practice for Youth and Community Development Work*. Exeter: Learning Matters.

Boyd, R. D. and Myers, J. G. (1988). Transformative education. *International Journal of Lifelong Education* 7(4): 261–284.

Brueggemaan, W. (1995). Preaching as reimagination. *Theology Today*, 52(3): 319–320.

Coburn, A. (2012). Learning about equality: A study of a generic youth work setting. Unpublished PhD thesis. Glasgow University of Strathclyde.

Coburn A. (2011). Liberation or containment: Paradoxes in youth work as a catalyst for powerful learning. *Journal of Youth and Policy* 106: 66–77.

Coburn, A. (2010). Youth work as border pedagogy. In J. Batsleer and B. Davies (Eds.), *What Is Youth Work?* (pp. 33–46). Exeter: Learning Matters.

Coburn, A. and Wallace, D., (2011). *Youth Work in Communities and Schools*. Edinburgh, Dunedin

Cohen, A. P. (1985). *The Symbolic Construction of Community*. London: Routledge.

Freire, P. (2007). *Pedagogy of Hope: Reliving Pedagogy of the Oppressed* (R. Barr, Trans.). London: Continuum.

Freire, P. (1996). *Pedagogy of the Oppressed* (M. B. Ramos, Trans.) (2nd ed.). London: Penguin.

Freire, P. (2005). *Teachers as Cultural Workers: Letters to Those Who Dare Teach*. Boulder: Westview Press.

Giroux, H. (2014). No bailouts for youth: Broken promises and dashed hopes. In A. Ibrahim and S. Steinberg (Eds.), *Critical Youth Studies Reader* (pp. 97–103). New York: Peter Lang.

Giroux, H. (2005). *Border Crossings: Cultural Workers and the Politics of Education*. Abingdon: Routledge.

Giroux, H. (2013). Challenging casino capitalism and authoritarian politics in the age of disposability. Accessed January 6, 2016, at http://www.truth-out.org/news/item/17176-henry-a-giroux-americas-education-deficit

Gramsci, A. (1999). *Selections from the Prison Notebooks of Antonio Gramsci*. (Q. Hoare and G Nowell-Smith, Trans.). Retrieved 29 April 29 2012 from http://www.walkingbutterfly.com/wp-content/uploads/2010/12/gramsci-prison-notebooksvol1.pdf

Harland, K. and McCready, S. (2012). *Taking boys seriously—A longitudinal study of adolescent male school-life experiences in Northern Ireland*. Jordanstown, University of Ulster: Department of Justice, Northern Ireland.

Kincheloe, J. (2008). *Critical Pedagogy*. New York: Peter Lang.

Illich, I. (1970). *Deschooling Society*. London: Marion Boyars.

Land, R., Cousin, G., Meyer, J. H. F. and Davies, P. (2005). Threshold concepts and troublesome knowledge (3): implications for course design and evaluation, In: C. Rust (ed.), Improving Student Learning - diversity and inclusivity, Proceedings of the 12th Improving Student Learning Conference. Oxford: Oxford Centre for Staff and Learning Development (OCSLD), pp. 53–64. ["https://www.ee.ucl.ac.uk/%7Emflanaga/ISL04-pp53-64-Land-et-al.pdf" http://www.ee.ucl.ac.uk/~mflanaga/ISL04-pp53-64-Land-et-al.pdf

Land, R., Meyer, J. H. F. and Baillie, C. (2010). *Threshold Concepts and Transformational Learning*. Rotterdam: Sense.

McLaren, P. (2009). Critical pedagogy: A look at the major concepts. In A. Darder, M. Baltodano, and R. Torres (Eds.), *The Critical Pedagogy Reader* (pp. 183–208). Oxon: Routledge.

Martin, I. (2007). Reclaiming social purpose: Framing the discussion. *The Edinburgh Papers*. Edinburgh: Edinburgh University.

Martin, I. (2001). Lifelong learning: For earning, yawning or yearning. *Adults Learning 13*(2): 14–17.

Maxton, G. and Randers, J. (2016). Reinventing prosperity: Managing economic growth to reduce unemployment, inequality and climate change. Vancouver: Greystone

Mezirow, J. (2009). An overview of transformative learning. In K. Illeris (Ed.), *Contemporary Theories of Learning: Learning Theorists in Their Own Words* (pp. 90–105). Oxon: Routledge.

Sen, A. (1985). Well-being, agency and freedom: The Dewey lectures 1984. *Journal of Philosophy 82*: 169–221. Retrieved 10 May 2016 from http://www.freelogy.org/w/images/d/dc/Sen85.pdf

Young, J. (2007). *The Vertigo of Late Modernity*. London: SAGE.

INDEX

Studies in Criticality

General Editor
Shirley R. Steinberg

Counterpoints publishes the most compelling and imaginative books being written in education today. Grounded on the theoretical advances in criticalism, feminism, and postmodernism in the last two decades of the twentieth century, Counterpoints engages the meaning of these innovations in various forms of educational expression. Committed to the proposition that theoretical literature should be accessible to a variety of audiences, the series insists that its authors avoid esoteric and jargonistic languages that transform educational scholarship into an elite discourse for the initiated. Scholarly work matters only to the degree it affects consciousness and practice at multiple sites. Counterpoints' editorial policy is based on these principles and the ability of scholars to break new ground, to open new conversations, to go where educators have never gone before.

For additional information about this series or for the submission of manuscripts, please contact:

Shirley R. Steinberg
c/o Peter Lang Publishing, Inc.
29 Broadway, 18th floor
New York, New York 10006

To order other books in this series, please contact our Customer Service Department:

(800) 770-LANG (within the U.S.)
(212) 647-7706 (outside the U.S.)
(212) 647-7707 FAX

Or browse online by series:
www.peterlang.com